Praise for *Reclaim Compassi*

MW00667045

"Lisa and Melissa are the leading voices in the foster and adoption community on all things blocked care, and *Reclaim Compassion* is their great gift to us. *Reclaim Compassion* provides a comprehensive and accessible explanation of the 'why' behind the blocked care that so many foster and adoptive parents experience and offers the hope of something better. The chapter reflections and practices alone have the potential to be truly life changing. Lisa's and Melissa's holistic brain, body, and spirit approach to understanding and overcoming blocked care will lead you to personal healing and meaningful connection with your children. Every foster and adoptive parent should read this book!"

—Jamie Finn
Director of Foster the Family
Author of *Foster the Family*

Reclaim Compassion practically and compassionately addresses part of parenting that no one wants to talk about. Lisa C. Qualls and Melissa Corkum are the go-to experts on blocked care, and this book is proof. No one understands it better than they do. We can't recommend this book enough!"

—Mike and Kristin Berry
Hosts of *The Honestly Adoption Podcast*
Coauthors of *Securely Attached*

"A must-read for the Christian adoptive parent who is struggling to like their child and doesn't know what to do. Lisa and Melissa help you find the compassion you need for yourself, so you can reclaim compassion for your child."

—Robyn Gobbel, LMSW-Clinical
Author of *Raising Kids with Big, Baffling Behaviors*

"Lisa and Melissa put into words what so many parents through adoption have experienced. In this book, you will feel seen, validated, and known. But the authors don't stop there. This book is full of practical applications, tools, and resources that will help restore your compassion for your children and yourself. If you feel like you're drowning, this book is exactly what you need."

—Joshua Hook, PhD, Professor of Psychology,
University of North Texas
—Jenn Ranter Hook, MA, Founder of Replanted Ministry
Coauthors of *Thriving Families*

"When I heard that Lisa and Melissa were working on a book on blocked care, I knew it would meet an incredible need. My expectations for this book have been met abundantly. Their honesty and vulnerability in opening this discussion provide a path of understanding that hasn't been a part of conversations within the adoption community in this practical way. It is a must-read. It will also be a great book for our future book clubs!"

—Jayne Schooler
Coauthor of *Wounded Children, Healing Homes;*
Telling the Truth to Your Adopted or Foster Child;
and *The Whole Life Adoption Book*

"Parenting is the hardest job on earth. What if a book could make it a little easier? Qualls and Corkum have woven the essentials of trauma and the brain into their heart for the adoptive family to create a gentle yet effective guide for parents. Christian moms and dads will find solace, solidarity, and hope within these pages as they move from the hopelessness and despair of blocked care to true healing in heart, mind, and spirit."

—Jessica Sinarski, LPCMH, Certified Adoption Therapist
Author of *Riley the Brave* and *Light Up the Learning Brain*

"I've never felt so seen or known in my parenting journey. *Reclaim Compassion*, along with Lisa's and Melissa's podcast, has helped me discover that I'm not broken as a mother or alone as an adoptive parent. This book will equip you with tools to heal and overcome a very real and painful part of many adoption parenting journeys. Adoptive parent, if you're here doing the work, you are not a monster, you can heal, and this book will be a huge part of that process."

—Whitney Runyon
Cofounder and Creative Director of The Archibald Project

"Lisa and Melissa do a fantastic job helping parents feel seen and heard in *Reclaim Compassion*. Weaving the narrative of real families struggling to connect with their kids allows readers to see themself while finding new hope for their families. *Reclaim Compassion* offers practical advice that parents need to navigate the adoption journey."

—Ryan and Kayla North
Cofounders of One Big Happy Home
Hosts of *The Empowered Parent Podcast*

RECLAIM COMPASSION

The Adoptive Parent's Guide to
Overcoming Blocked Care
with Neuroscience and Faith

LISA C. QUALLS

MELISSA CORKUM

AW
ADOPTION WISE PRESS

Some names and recognizable details have been changed to protect the privacy of those who have shared their stories for this book.

The information in this book is intended solely as an educational resource, not a tool to be used for medical diagnosis or treatment. The information presented is in no way a substitute for consultation with a personal health care professional. Readers should consult their personal health care professional before adopting any of the suggestions in this book or drawing inferences from the text. The authors and publisher specifically disclaim responsibility for any liability, loss, or risk, personal or otherwise, which is incurred as a consequence, directly or indirectly, of the use of and/or application of the contents of this book.

Published by Adoption Wise Press

ISBN Paperback 979-8-9877643-1-2
ISBN Ebook 979-8-9877643-0-5

Design and composition by Leah Kent
Cover design by Leah Kent

For Kay.

And for all the adoptive parents who have invited me to be their companion on this winding road.

—Lisa

For my parents, who loved and raised us well despite having no post-adoption support.

—Melissa

CONTENTS

Introduction

We're so glad you're here. You've picked up this book because something in your relationship with your child doesn't feel right. Parenting seems extra difficult and less rewarding than you ever imagined. But take heart—you'll find hope and healing in the strategies, stories, and solutions we offer.

We wrote this book because we know what it's like to feel excited and hopeful when adopting new children, only to grow increasingly discouraged by challenging behaviors and lack of connection. We've each lost sight of our compassion on our parenting journeys and why we even wanted to adopt in the first place.

Over the years, as we scrambled to parent our kids with attachment struggles and challenging behaviors, we tried everything. We read books, got on social media, sought professional help, and talked to anyone who might have answers. It seemed like nothing was working, our families were falling apart, and we were only becoming more stressed and exhausted. We knew God had something better for us, our kids, and our families, but we couldn't seem to find our way back to the parents we wanted to be.

Today, between the two of us, we represent all three parts of the adoption triad and are moms to eighteen kids. We've been around the block a couple times with kids by birth, adoption, and foster care, and we want you to know we've been where you are and lived to tell about it. It's possible to rebuild your compassion and enjoy parenting again.

As nationally recognized post-adoption support specialists with extensive training in trauma-informed practices, connected parenting, and nervous-system care, we've also seen firsthand the debilitating effect that feelings of discouragement, shame, or resentment can have on parents when they don't know how to get past the struggles. On its own, the discouragement parents experience can slide down into despair.

In response to one of Lisa's posts on her parenting blog years ago, a reader reached out to her for help, admitting to a painful sentiment that we've come to see is all too common. The reader shared:

> "How have you overcome any bad feelings you have toward your adopted kids who have so many challenging behaviors? I ask because I am TRYING to attach to my six-year-old adopted daughter, but her behavior just makes me really not like her at all. She has been home almost a year, and I feel like we are just stuck in this rut and I am just giving up. I'm only tolerating her until she turns eighteen!"

Other readers rushed in with their responses, many saying they had never felt they could be truly honest about their feelings. They expressed being ashamed of their inability to really like their kids. Do any of these comments from other parents feel familiar to resonate with you?

> "I spend a lot of time struggling with this child's behaviors, and I grieve the fact that I don't 'feel the like.' I spend so much time wondering what is wrong with me."

> "I have been struggling to attach to my eleven-year-old adopted daughter for three years now. I wake up each day hoping this will be the day we turn a corner. But I have just recently admitted to myself that I really don't like her most of the time. To make things worse, it was love and attachment at first sight with her thirteen-year-old brother. I continually beat myself up for being such a terrible person . . . who doesn't like their own child? Thanks to you and others in our position, I am realizing I'm not alone."

> "I am really struggling to find positive feelings for this child. I know he needs my love and care, and I think we are caring for him well and providing much-needed stability. But I do not like him. I'm embarrassed to even type it. He annoys me, whines constantly, and wakes multiple times a night."

> "I find myself praying for his reunification—not for his positive future, but to get him out of my house!"

> "My son is six and has been with us for only seven months. But I am at a low feeling of guilt and discouragement because I do not love him like my two bio kids. It is so awful to say, but he irritates me constantly. I feel like my blood pressure must be going through the roof because even when my words are patient, and I have a smile on my face, I am about to bubble over. . . . Mostly I

> wonder, though, will it get better? I used to be so happy and at peace with my family. I used to be so happy with myself as a mother. I want that back."

Lisa's original discussion had struck a raw nerve, uncovering a painful but real experience shared by many parents—including herself—who were ashamed and bewildered by their feelings. What stands out to us in these responses is each parent's overwhelming feeling of something being wrong and their struggle with the accompanying shame that comes with it. They're expressing that they no longer feel like themselves or never imagined parenting would be like this. A decade later, the post that triggered all the comments remains as one of the most popular on the blog, and we've seen in our work with parents over the years that the same heartaches and difficulties are no less relevant today. We also know the challenges are not due to poor parenting or lack of trying.

Like the commenters on Lisa's blog, Melissa had, years ago, similarly experienced a season of being so tired she wanted to give up. But in her search to better understand herself and become a more effective parent, she came across a book called *Brain-Based Parenting*, by Daniel A. Hughes and Jonathan Baylin. She loved how the authors used neuroscience, the study of the brain and the rest of the nervous system, to explain behaviors. Her attention was particularly drawn to the chapter on blocked care, and she called Lisa, who cried tears of relief to learn that blocked care was an actual thing.

We realized that before we even knew it had a name, we had seen signs of blocked care in ourselves and in the parents we served. And at long last, we finally had words and science to explain our experiences.

Blocked care is a self-protective mechanism in the nervous system activated by excessive stress. This suppresses the higher brain functions needed for caregiving, causing your nervous system to develop a defensive stance toward your child.[1] Your heart seems to have left the relationship. But there is good news: you can overcome blocked care and find your way back to the parent you long to be. We're proof of it, as are the thousands of parents we've served.

This book is for you if:

- you knew your child had trauma, but you feel like you're in over your head.
- you started this parenting process hopeful and enthusiastic, but now you can hardly get out of bed in the morning.
- you thought you were a great parent, but now you feel like a failure.
- you wanted to help a child, but they don't seem to want you at all.
- your friends and family were excited and supportive at first, but now it seems you're in this alone.
- you had so much love to give, but now you find it hard to even like your child.

- life feels like it will never be the same, and you wonder where God is.

We created this book to validate your experience, show you how blocked care happens, and help you come out on the other side.

How to Read This Book

Reclaim Compassion is divided into three parts:

> Part 1 is an exploration of what you experienced after bringing your child into your family. Is your experience different from what you expected? Are you struggling with shame? Are there losses that need to be acknowledged and grieved? We'll guide you through it.
>
> Part 2 dives into the neuroscience of blocked trust and blocked care. We'll answer the question, "How did this happen?" As we often tell parents, there are logical reasons as to why it's so hard to keep caring. We can't wait for you to learn all about it.
>
> Part 3 is a plan for recovery. We'll introduce you to a greater understanding of neuroscience and show you how to care practically for your nervous system. We'll lead you through an exploration of your internal world, external world, and relational world, with the purpose of renewing compassion for your child and yourself.

The chapters are intended to be read in order, one chapter per week. Each one ends with suggested daily practices for you to follow. Don't worry—we kept them short and sweet because we know your life is already full, and you are tired. The practices are designed to begin easing the shame and sorrow of blocked care, and though they will require a small investment of time from you, we believe you're worth it and will see a difference.

This book can also be read with a group of parents working together toward healing or shared with family members or friends who hope to gain a better understanding of what you're going through.

As followers of Christ, we reference our faith throughout the book. God's living presence and steadfast love has carried us through the hardest seasons of our lives. We believe He is our source of hope, and we are profoundly grateful to Him. That being said, this book is for everyone. The daily practices, information on the brain and neuroscience, and strategies for overcoming blocked care are powerful and effective for healing. If you aren't a person of faith, you will still find a path for overcoming blocked care, one that offers you hope and help.

We want to caution you that reading this book could bring up feelings you've held in for a long time or past trauma that you've never had a chance to address before. You may find yourself overwhelmed. When possible, read this with a trusted friend, spouse, therapist, or support person and process it with them along the way. And read it at your own pace—even if you need to go slower—taking breaks when you need them. The most important thing to us is that you find the information, healing, and restoration you need.

A final word: If you have reached the point in which you truly feel you can't go on as a parent or you fear you could hurt yourself or your child, we urge you to seek professional help by calling a crisis line or reaching out to a therapist. We understand it may be frightening, but there are too many instances in the fostering and adoption community in which despair has resulted in tragedy. Know that you are very much loved, and there is hope and help available.

A Note to Adoptees from Melissa

As a school-aged child, I raged for hours about chores. I screamed, cried, slammed doors, and kicked walls. My mom did her best with what she knew, but there were no trauma-informed parenting books or groups of supportive adoptive families on social media available to her at that time. I wish she'd had safe people to share her exhaustion and feelings of helplessness with—other parents who never doubted that she loved me but validated how hard it was to navigate such big behaviors. Any resources for her would have also benefited my siblings and me.

We share the stories of parents in this book, so other parents will feel safer exploring their experiences and starting the journey of overcoming blocked care. Reading their comments may bring up anger or shame for you, and you may feel that we're placing adoptive parents at the center of the adoption experience and forgetting the perspective of the child. But at the heart of it all, we care so deeply for the child that we're committed to increasing awareness and providing resources for parents. We believe every adoptee should experience compassionate and connected parenting, free from blocked care.

Pre-reading Assessment

Before you get started, take a moment to fill out a pre-assessment and see where you are at the beginning of your journey. The items in the post-assessment at the end of the book are identical to these, offering you a consistent way to gauge how far you've progressed by the time you've finished reading.

Please respond with one of the following: 1—Never, 2—Rarely, 3—Sometimes, 4—Often, 5—Always

I'm too caught up in coping with my child's behavior to be curious about the meaning behind it.	1	2	3	4	5
I feel defensive and guard myself from rejection.	1	2	3	4	5
I feel burned out, chronically overwhelmed, and fatigued.	1	2	3	4	5
I feel resentment toward one or more of my children or my situation as a whole. I may even regret adopting or fostering.	1	2	3	4	5
I feel irritable with other family and friends.	1	2	3	4	5
I isolate myself.	1	2	3	4	5
I'm cynical about helpful ideas.	1	2	3	4	5

I've lost compassion, which has led to shame.	1 2 3 4 5
I've experienced a crisis of faith or challenge of a personal belief system.	1 2 3 4 5
I don't feel real pleasure in parenting.	1 2 3 4 5

PART 1:
The Experience of Blocked Care

Amanda loved being a mom. When she and Sam married after college graduation, they dreamed of having a large family. By their tenth anniversary, they had two daughters, ages six and eight, and a four-year-old son. When they learned of the need for foster parents in their community, they decided to become licensed to foster and thought they might one day adopt. After their first few foster placements, their social worker approached them about two young boys in the foster care system who were available for adoption. Amanda and Sam were thrilled to be selected as the permanent placement. Finally, they would have the large family they'd always dreamed of.

They knew the boys had experienced adversity in their short lives. Fortunately, Amanda and Sam had read all of the recommended books and attended a couple of highly recommended weekend training events for adoptive and foster parents. Amanda even joined some Facebook groups for foster and adoptive moms.

When the boys first arrived, it seemed like everything was going pretty well, with the exception of sleep. One of their sons hardly slept at all, which meant Amanda found herself perpetually exhausted. But as the weeks went on, things began to get worse. Their son started getting very upset over seemingly small things. His crying turned into meltdowns, unlike any she'd seen before. And he became aggressive toward his siblings. It got to where Amanda felt as if she had entered a war zone.

She pulled out the adoption books she had previously read and scanned them for help. She also posted in a Facebook group and got lots of encouraging advice. Amanda understood from her research that her son wasn't a bad kid but rather was acting out of fear due to early adverse experiences. She knew she had to keep focusing on building trust with him and helping him heal, and she found a trauma-informed therapist to work with their family.

When her son was upset, he said he hated her, and it seemed to her to be true. But she continued to be loving toward her son, even though he seemed to reject her over and over again. Amanda was working harder to parent than she ever had before.

As the months passed, the angry words from her son hurt less. She became more used to his verbal assaults; in fact, she was better able to let them roll off her and wouldn't let them pierce her heart as she had before. If she tried to give her son affection and he pushed her away, she would tell herself it didn't matter.

But even though she tried to not let him affect her, Amanda found herself feeling anxious when she heard him waking in the morning. She still hoped one day everything would be better. She fed him well, participated in therapy, met with teachers, and took good care of him. But her heart just wasn't in it anymore. She realized she was counting the years until he would graduate from high school and move away to college.

Sometimes, Amanda wondered who she had become and how she had gotten there. How could a mother not like her child? She felt ashamed that she just wanted him to go away. She didn't think anyone would understand, so she kept all these thoughts and her feelings to herself, feeling stuck and hopeless.

Why Does a Parent's Heart Shut Down?

Like Amanda, many parents we work with through our post-adoption services get to this place of apathy toward their child. They still love them, but liking and enjoying them has become exceedingly difficult.

When we prompt parents to be honest, and they realize they can trust us, they will put words to it. One mom told us,

> "We adopted our daughter from foster care when she was two years old. We believed she just needed love, and all would be right in the world. We soon learned that no amount of love and care would be enough, and it still isn't, and she is almost

> seventeen. The shame I feel for not liking her has been debilitating. Being in the same room with her makes my stomach tighten, and I get nauseated. I love her very much but have pretended to like her for years. Thank you for letting me know that I am not alone!"

But most of the time, these parents stay silent and withdrawn. The shame they feel is overwhelming, and it leads to a sense of isolation and feelings of despair.

Why does this happen? Why does a parent, who loves their kids and is doing their very best, find that their heart has simply shut down toward their child?

To get to that, we'll first need to take a close look at ourselves in Part 1.

Chapter 1: Recognize Your Motivations and Expectations

Before you begin the process of reclaiming compassion for yourself and your child, it's helpful to reflect on the series of events that brought you to this place. We'll get to what happened in your nervous system, but before we do, we ask you to explore your motivations and expectations for adopting.

Motivations

Think of something hard you've done in your life, not something that happened to you, but something you chose to do. Maybe it was getting a degree or running a race. Maybe you decided to start a business. Maybe you've even done something really hard, like getting sober or bringing your marriage back from the brink of divorce.

In every case, something prompted you to consider the goal, and it was powerful enough to move you to make sacrifices to make it happen. Maybe the action you had to take required you to establish a budget, work while taking classes, or learn how to manage employees. Maybe your goal required daily meetings and saying no to things you had previously relied on. Or maybe getting to where you needed to be took months of weekly counseling appointments with your husband. Whatever it was and whatever it took—you decided it was worth the sacrifice.

Now let's talk about adoption. Typically, adoption doesn't just happen; it takes a huge commitment and loads of determination to jump through all the hoops and fill out stacks of documents. Coming up with the required amount of money is no small task either. But you did it. You traveled around the globe, or maybe just across town, and you adopted your child.

We would venture to guess if you're reading this book that adoption has been hard, likely even much harder than you expected. You may wonder how everything could have gone so wrong. You may doubt you were cut out for this. And while you may not say it out loud, you may wonder if you made a huge mistake.

Think back to the very beginning. For some of you, you'll be thinking back several years. For others, you may need to go all the way back to your childhood. When was the seed of adoption planted in your heart? What happened to make the seed grow? What sacrifices did you make to bring your child home? We imagine you made lots of them. You must have believed adopting your child was very important.

You may have adopted because you had a strong sense of justice, or it was simply the right thing to do. You may have felt moved by the suffering of children living in difficult circumstances. You may have experienced infertility and chosen adoption to grow your family. Or you may have thought adopting would be an adventure, and you were up for the challenge.

Here are our stories of how we came to adopt:

> **Melissa**
> Our adoption journey started with my husband, Patrick. He had known from a young age that he wanted to adopt. On our first date, he said two things to me: "I'm dating to find a wife, so if at any point you know you can't marry me, let me know," and "I know I want to adopt, so are you okay with that?" I couldn't yet say that I knew Patrick was the one for me, but as an adoptee wired to always see the bright side of things, I figured I couldn't be against adoption.
>
> After getting married and having two kids by birth, when our thoughts about adoption turned to action, we felt called by God to provide a home for children who were harder to place—due to special needs or age—and were already waiting for families.

> **Lisa**
> I had always been passionate about caring for children in need. I went to college to get a degree that would let me work with kids, but I didn't think I would become an

> adoptive mom. The seed of adoption was planted in me when a close friend called to tell me she and her husband were adopting two little boys from Ethiopia. Hearing this, it felt like God opened a door so wide that we hardly had to pick up our feet to walk through. After that, I could not stop reading about adoption, praying about adoption, and reading blogs about it.
>
> When my husband Russ and I finally decided to move forward with it, I was a fiercely determined woman, filling out paperwork at a rate that surprised everyone. Our plan had been to adopt two little boys. It was a good and sensible plan, but God had something else in mind. In the end, we adopted two little boys and a little girl in 2007 and returned to Ethiopia to adopt another daughter a year later.

When we reflect back, we are reminded of our original motivations. For Melissa, it was to provide a home for a child who was harder to place. For Lisa, it was to embrace a child who needed the love and care of a family. We both also believed we were fulfilling God's exhortation to care for orphans. It was helpful for us to identify our motivations in order to refresh our resolve to be the best parents we could be, even when we were discouraged and experiencing blocked care.

Can you remember back to the very beginning of your story? You had a compelling reason. What comes to mind?

Here are some of the motivations other parents have shared with us:

> "If you're a really good Christian, you're going to do this thing."

> "I just wanted to help kids in need, in foster care. We now know that does not always go so well because you're not always able to help in the ways that you imagine yourself being able to help."

> "We were ready to be parents and, you know, there were kids that needed families. And so, okay, we'll do it. I mean, we really didn't overthink it."

> "We felt like we were self-centered thirty-somethings. We realized we needed to move on and begin this family. So that's how we got there."

> "This is hard to admit, but I felt that if I only adopted once, that I wasn't really an advocate, or I wasn't really a believer of adoption. I felt that to be a really committed person to adoption, I need to do it twice."

Again, understanding your motivations for adoption is important because it may help you persevere. You may also discover your initial motivations no longer hold meaning. This may require you to explore new motivations that inspire you to press on.

Expectations

Have you ever had one of those moments when you wonder, "What have I done to my family?", "What have I done to my marriage?", or "What have I done to my life?" We have, and we're here to tell you that you're not alone.

Like us, you had expectations of what life would be like as an adoptive parent, but your relationship with your child may be turning out differently than you expected. Reflecting on the gap between your expectations and your reality can shed insight on why blocked care happens.

> **Melissa**
> When my husband and I adopted in 2009, our agency's required training focused on two things: children with institutional behaviors and parenting transracially. We blew through our adoption training because our son hadn't spent time in an institution, and he wasn't going to be the only Korean in our family. I also saw myself as a happy adoptee, so I naively thought I could raise happy adoptees. Because I had lived the adoptee life and knew what it was like, I didn't feel I needed a training to tell me how to parent an adoptee.
>
> Our son came home like a human tornado. I think he had opened every drawer and cabinet and pushed every button in our house within an hour of being home. As time went on, I realized I had zero tools other than yelling and timeouts, which had worked just fine with our first two kids. It didn't take long for me to start feeling powerless and frustrated. Every morning, when I would hear his steps thundering down the hall, I would cringe and wonder why we had thought this was such a good idea. It didn't help that anyone who didn't live with him thought he was the cutest kid ever, and people were always joking about taking him home with them. This added to the sense of shame I already felt.
>
> When we adopted three unrelated older children from Ethiopia in 2012, we thought we were more prepared, especially because earlier that year, we had learned

about connected parenting and even become Empowered to Connect parent trainers. You would've thought I'd have learned after our first experience that it wouldn't be so easy, but as new parent trainers, I had also renewed my expectation that we had the skills and knowledge we needed. We expected our children to respond positively to our attempts at connection, but we underestimated our children's drive for self-protection, which made it incredibly difficult for them to develop secure attachment to us. Eventually, we had to seek out long-term respite for one of our kids. Then our oldest two packed their suitcases at the ages of 16 and 17 and left for Job Corps, a residential education and job training program, with no intention of returning home.

For my husband and I, our family—and hearts—felt broken in every way. In terms of my expectations of adoption, there was a big gap between what I thought our family would be and what our reality was. It turns out, on top of everything else, I had unknowingly suppressed fears of abandonment and rejection from my experience of being left on an orphanage doorstep as a newborn. Those fears chose the not-so-opportune time to rear their ugly head as I tried to parent our Ethiopian teenagers, only to be rejected by them again and again.

Dr. Karyn Purvis, Lisa's coauthor of the popular book, *The Connected Parent: Real-Life Strategies for Building Trust and Attachment*, wasn't joking when she said, "To bring a child to a place of healing, you must know the path yourself."[1] I never expected this journey to require so much processing of my own history in order to improve the relationships with my children.

Lisa

When we added four children to our family through adoption, I fully expected it to be a tough transition. Our new children were leaving behind everything they knew in life up to that point, and they had every reason to be frightened. We felt it was important to help them feel safe, and I was confident we could do it. After all, we had been parents for 20 years and were good at it.

I won't say caring for our kids was always easy, but I truly loved being a mom. My husband and I were not perfect parents, but we were good parents who loved Jesus and loved our children. We knew we had something beautiful, and we wanted to share it with children who needed a family.

In 2007, we traveled to Ethiopia to bring our three young children home. It quickly became apparent to us that one of our new daughters was a very high energy, challenging child. As the days passed, our concern over our daughter grew, and we knew we were likely to have a difficult time when we got home.

We soon learned that fear doesn't always look like we think it should. Our daughter's fear emerged as out-of-control rages, screaming, and hurting her siblings. Our little ones began hiding in the closet when the screaming started, and nobody felt safe in our home. I was scared and at a loss. Nothing we knew about parenting had prepared me for this level of chaos.

Prior to our daughter coming home, I had expected I would be a good and loving mom, and because of my love and hard work, this would be enough to help my

> children heal from any past wounds. Instead, there were many tears at our house, including mine. No matter how hard I tried to build connection, nothing seemed to ease her fear. The resulting behaviors made it difficult to keep trying. Many days, I felt like a failure.
>
> The gap between what I expected and my reality was vast.

We've seen, over the years, that though every family situation is unique, many of the effects of blocked care and ensuing feelings around them are not. Our expectations as parents played a role in the struggles and emotions we faced.

Other parents have echoed similar sentiments, telling us:

> "Because of the enormous amount of attention and therapeutic parenting our son needs, he is going to be our one and only—there was a time when we thought we would bring a brother or sister home, but not anymore. There are days I feel cheated out of the 'real' mommy experience—the one where your child is attached to you without you having to fight for it."

> "I never thought I would struggle with liking the child God had so providentially given me."

> "I had checked all the boxes of things I thought we needed to know. I had researched until I thought we were prepared. Apparently, I was wrong."

> "I want meaningful connection with all my children. I know they're young, but you can still have deep relationships and meaningful relationships with children. Particularly in our last adoption, I feel a disconnect that there is not a meaningful connection. The

> connection I want to have is not what she wants to have, but I'm trying to find ways to connect to her because of this gap for me."
>
> "The lack of tranquility and peace, and the stressful interactions in my home was so stressful. Keeping all of that inside really rocked my boat."
>
> "I am sure I thought I had everything within my own capacity to do whatever was needed. It took us getting to a really hard place, like a pretty dark place in our family, before we even thought we needed support and humbled ourselves enough to go and get it. It was a big gap."

We know that the gap between your expectations and reality can cause feelings of shame, fear, or resentment. Parenting has a way of bringing our weaknesses and sinfulness bubbling to the surface. We can run from the discomfort, blame everyone around us, or soothe the pain in unhealthy ways. Or we can embrace parenting as the holy and sanctifying work it is, and let God overhaul our hearts.

We believe God is always at work in our lives. He uses people and circumstances to teach us and open our hearts to ways He can use us. The Holy Spirit speaks to us in ways we can't explain and stirs our hearts. Remember who you are. As a child of God, you can trust that your life is not a collection of random events. God has a plan and is intentionally working to lead you in ways to help you become more like Him and put His love on display to the world. Remember these truths when you feel the most defeated.

Reflections and Practices for Chapter 1

Day 1: Find Joy

This week, we want you to focus on intentionally finding joy.

In her book, *Attaching in Adoption*, Deborah D. Gray writes about self-care tools for parents who are weary or burned-out from the needs of their children. She writes, “When parents have begun to be too worn out, it is often because they have spent too much time doing tasks and have deleted the fun or enjoyable things in their life.”[2] She gives a list of favorite suggestions from parents in her practice. We call this simple practice Fifty Points of Joy.

This week, we invite you to make a list of items that bring you joy. These can be big things, like getting a massage or going out to dinner. They can also be small things, such as lighting a candle or sipping your favorite tea. This list should continue growing over the coming weeks as you think of more things to add. Each day, try to complete seven or eight points of joy, putting checkmarks next to them as you go. Try to get fifty check marks on the list each week. Feel free to check off the same item more than once in a day or even across multiple days. If it brings you joy, it absolutely counts!

Imagine how this will renew your hope and strength, intentionally drawing your attention and focus each day to the things that feed your soul and fill your heart. It may be hard to do at first, but we’ve found this practice to be powerful for renewing hope and compassion in our own lives and in the lives of the parents we work with.

Here are some examples from Melissa's list:

1. Taking a morning walk.
2. Drinking a cup of ginger tea.
3. Smelling a citrus essential oil.
4. Eating something salty and crunchy.
5. Drinking grapefruit-flavored sparkling water and eating popcorn while watching a movie with Patrick.
6. Reading a novel.
7. Texting a friend a note of encouragement.
8. Going out to a farm-to-table restaurant.
9. Hanging out with friends.
10. Going to bed in clean sheets.

And here are examples from Lisa's list:

1. Sitting on the front porch for five minutes with a mug of tea or coffee.
2. Lighting a candle on my bathroom counter as I get ready in the morning.
3. Listening to an audiobook or podcast while cooking.
4. Getting together with a friend for an hour.
5. Putting a vase of flowers on the kitchen counter.
6. Taking my dog for a walk.
7. Watching a movie that makes me laugh.
8. Reading a book for pleasure—not adoption related!
9. Taking a few extra minutes at bedtime to put a favorite essential oil in my diffuser.
10. Video chatting with my adult kids and grandbabies.

As you can see, we're not talking about complicated or expensive moments of joy. Most of these are small moments or simple acts woven into our daily lives. When you're in the midst of a hard day and just trying to make it through, joy is probably not the overwhelming feeling you have. But identifying what brings you joy and intentionally creating space for it in simple ways is a gift you can give yourself. From a physiological standpoint, intentionally adding joy back into your day can calm your nervous system, which can help you feel more compassionate and kind toward yourself. We can't change our kids' behaviors or their reactions to us, but we can change the way we care for ourselves.

Day 2: Explore Your Motivations

Today, you will explore why you chose to adopt or do foster care. As we discussed in the chapter, it's important to reflect in order to make sense of how you're feeling now.

Check all that apply and/or add other motivations you had:

- ☐ You wanted to help a child.
- ☐ You wanted to grow your family.
- ☐ You went to an adoption event and felt moved to adopt.
- ☐ You experienced infertility and decided to adopt.
- ☐ You wanted to keep a sibling group together.
- ☐ You wanted to make your spouse happy.
- ☐ You always wanted to adopt—even as a young child.
- ☐ You said yes to kinship care.
- ☐ You knew it was simply the right thing to do.
- ☐ ______________________________
- ☐ ______________________________
- ☐ ______________________________
- ☐ ______________________________

Let's go deeper. We want you to remember the first moment when you knew you were going to adopt. How did you know it was meant to be? What happened? How did you feel? Write out your narrative or share it with a friend. Or do both! This can bring clarity, especially if you're feeling overwhelmed and discouraged.

Day 3: Recognize the Gap

Heads up: today's practice may be a tough one. We want you to fill out this chart comparing your expectations of life after adopting to your actual life now.

Expectations	Reality

As you look at the chart, what do you feel? Take a few moments to write about your emotions. If you find this difficult, search online for a feelings wheel for helpful suggestions. We'll process this more when we address grief in Chapter 2.

Day 4: Renew Your Inspiration

After yesterday's practice, you may feel discouraged or like you want to give up. Today is about finding new inspiration. Lamentations 3:21–22 (ESV) says,

> "But this I call to mind, and therefore I have hope: The steadfast love of the Lord never ceases; his mercies never come to an end."

The Word tells us we can choose to call to mind that which gives us hope. We can reflect on the ways God has helped us, rescued us, and given us joy even amid hardship.

We asked adoptive parents to share the Bible verses they find most helpful. One parent wrote:

> "Some days, it's 'Jesus wept' (John 11:35 NKJV), which helps me know I'm not alone. Other days, it's 'I can do all things through Christ who strengthens me' (Phil. 4:13 NKJV), which is the verse in the Bible with the most impact for me. Jesus felt emotions, and God wants us to process and feel them too. I love that."

Another wrote:

> "This verse makes me teary. Our kids' stories aren't over. There is hope. I have felt hopeless over two of my kids, and this has breathed new life back into me. I wrote it down and stuck it by my kitchen sink. . . . 'The Lord bless you and keep you; The Lord make His face shine upon you, And be gracious to you; The Lord lift up His countenance upon you, And give you peace' (Num. 6:24–26 NKJV)."

Here are some additional verses parents have shared with us; we hope they inspire hope, reminding you of how God loves you and is both with you and for you:

> "And the Lord, He is the One who goes before you. He will be with you, He will not leave you nor forsake you; do not fear nor be dismayed" (Deut. 31:8 NKJV).

> "Then I can boast in the day of Christ that I didn't run or labor for nothing. But even if I am poured out as a drink offering on the sacrificial service of your faith, I am glad and rejoice with all of you. In the same way you should also be glad and rejoice with me" (Phil. 2:16b–18 CSB).

> "When anxiety was great within me, your consolation brought me joy" (Ps. 94:19 NIV).

> "The Lord is my strength and my shield; my heart trusts in him, and he helps me. My heart leaps for joy, and with my song I praise him" (Ps. 28:7 NIV).

> "Let us not grow weary of doing good, for in due season we will reap, if we do not give up" (Gal. 6:9 ESV).

> "God is my refuge and strength, an ever-present help in trouble. Therefore we will not fear, though the earth give way and the mountains fall into the heart of the sea" (Ps. 46: 1–2 NIV).

"Cast your burden on the Lord, and he will sustain you; he will never permit the righteous to be moved" (Ps. 55:22 ESV).

" . . . 'Be strong and courageous, and do the work. Don't be afraid or discouraged, for the Lord God, my God, is with you. He won't leave you or abandon you . . . '" (1 Chron. 28:20 CSB).

"Therefore we do not lose heart. Though outwardly we are wasting away, yet inwardly we are being renewed day by day. For our light and momentary troubles are achieving for us an eternal glory that far outweighs them all. So we fix our eyes not on what is seen, but on what is unseen, since what is seen is temporary, but what is unseen is eternal" (2 Cor. 4:16–18 NIV).

"Peace I leave with you. My peace I give to you. I do not give to you as the world gives. Don't let your heart be troubled or fearful" (John 14:27 CSB).

"He restores my soul. He leads me in paths of righteousness for his name's sake" (Ps. 23:3 ESV).

"So do not fear, for I am with you; do not be dismayed, for I am your God. I will strengthen you and help you; I will uphold you with my righteous right hand" (Is. 41:10 NIV).

Which verses resonate with you? Choose one or two that challenge and encourage you to press on, regardless of your circumstances.

Write them here or post them where you'll notice them throughout your day.

Day 5: Read and Reflect

The weekly practices for each chapter end with a Read and Reflect exercise. Take your time and read the passage as many times as you like. Then, journal your reflections.

> "Jesus, our trust, your Gospel brings with it such a fine hope that we would like to give ourselves to the very end in order to follow you. And irresistibly the question arises: Where is the source of such hope? It lies in surrendering ourselves to you, Christ."[3]

Chapter 2:
Acknowledge Shame and Grief

Once parents consider their original motivations and expectations, shame and grief often bubble to the surface. You may also be feeling shame or grief about your lack of compassion toward your child.

Shame

No one wants to admit they really don't like being a parent or don't like their kids. When parents finally get honest, they are often overcome by feelings of shame and guilt. One mom reached out to us, saying, "I hate myself and who I have become. From loving mother to worst mother in the world. I dread each day, and I am so shut down. I don't know what to do anymore."

Shame is a hard, painful thing to experience. It makes us feel like there is something deeply wrong with us and affects our sense of worth. It feeds on secrecy, isolation, and unrealistic expectations, and it's a place where our insecurities seem to grow like weeds. Shame tells us we're alone and nobody could possibly understand. Or if someone could truly see what we're experiencing, we would be judged and rejected by them.

If you're experiencing shame, you may find yourself trying to hide yourself away because the risk of your struggle being exposed is terrifying. But God longs to reach into those dark places you are guarding so closely and flood them with compassion. Your deepest healing will come in receiving the abundance of His steadfast love for you.

The safest place we know is in God's presence. He is looking on you with the eyes of a loving Father. He knows your thoughts, your fears, and your failures, and He calls you His child.

Another key to overcoming shame is having a safe place to be vulnerable about your adoption journey—both the highs and the lows of it. To be able to say what you're feeling and know that others feel it too offers a sense of relief. Be assured, you are not alone. Here are some comments and messages we've received over time that show parents in the midst of their struggles:

> "I have been asking for the last five years, 'Is this the year I will love my adopted girls?' What's wrong with me? Everyone thinks they are great but me. Please help. I need someone to talk to."

> "I never thought I could have all the dark thoughts I have had at times over the years while parenting children from hard places. As parents, we need to band together and support one another

through the hard times, with honesty and prayer and understanding."

"We adopted our son from foster care when he was two years old. He is my grand-nephew, so this is a kinship adoption. At first, we thought he was just a little different—I can't even explain his strange behavior. We believed he just needed love and all would be right in the world. We soon learned no amount of love and care would be enough, and it still isn't, and he is almost seventeen. The shame I feel for not liking him has been debilitating."

"My older kids have seen a mom they didn't know existed. I pray they remember the happy, calm mom they once had. I pray someday we will all look back and see the refining and the good that came from our adoption experience. Right now, it's all just a little too ugly to have perspective."

"I thought I was the only one who had these dark thoughts and regrets. Our family has gone through hell and back a few times in the past three years. It doesn't seem to stop. I'm just now at the place to seek help. I hate that I'm not the mom I used to be, and it hurts so deeply when my bio kids tell me they want their mom back."

When parents learn they're not alone and what they're experiencing has a name, we watch the shame melt away:

"I feel very guilty about the feelings I have had about my child, and more so, the feelings I don't have. It is such a relief to know I am not alone and there is an explanation!"

"The commiseration of other parents brought me out of the depths and into finding comfort in my new self-image. I may never again live up to what I thought was a good mom, but I'm a more loving, compassionate, and engaged person in the world, and I understand God a whole lot more."

> **Lisa**
>
> Shame had a grip on me until I finally chose to be truly honest about our family's struggles. I'd been afraid to seek help because I didn't want people to know I was failing as an adoptive mom. I also didn't want them to know just how bad things were in our home. Our life had been shaken, and we weren't on solid ground. I was afraid, and I cried many tears during this time.
>
> On one particularly hard day, a friend happened to stop by. She and her husband had recently adopted two children, but their adjustment was going much better than ours. I stepped out onto the front porch where I could talk more freely, but I could hardly speak. Covering my face with my hands, I said through my tears, "I don't think I can go on." I told her about my hopelessness and the struggle to like my child. She hugged me and said, "I understand. Some days I feel the same way." Her empathy let me walk out of my place of darkness and into the light.

Grief

Grief is commonly associated with tangible losses, such as the death of a loved one. There are also losses related to infertility, the hellos and goodbyes of foster care, or expected adoptions that weren't completed.

Additionally, there are many unexpected losses when life changes dramatically after you add children to your family through adoption. If these losses aren't acknowledged, you may experience big emotions and not know why.

We've learned that anytime we experience a significant gap between our expectations and our reality, there's something we need to grieve. It helps to understand that there are different types of grief and loss. Ambiguous loss, common in adoption, is experienced when it's highly unlikely a person will reach emotional closure or have a clear understanding of the situation.[1] Disenfranchised grief is experienced when a loss is not easily recognized and may even seem invisible to others.[2]

These can be hard to understand, but we see them play out all the time. So that you can see how they might look, here are some examples of ambiguous or disenfranchised losses in Melissa's adoption story, as both an adoptee and adoptive parent:

- **Loss of birth family and culture**—This was part of the reality I faced when I was adopted internationally and interracially. It was not recognized until I was an adult. Additionally, the loss of my birth family remains ambiguous since I never know if reunion will be in our future.

- **Loss of belonging**—Ironically, I didn't experience this until I realized I was processing my adoption story differently than many other adoptees on social media. I often don't feel like I belong in the adoptee community.

- **Loss of normalcy**—We didn't expect the needs of our kids to impact so many of our daily routines.

- **Loss of safety**—With rages consuming 10 to 15 hours a week, I was always on edge, and our youngest son wanted to lock his bedroom door at night.

- **Loss of friends, church, community, and extended family**—We had a messy situation in which a family member tried to emancipate one of our kids from us and another situation in which a pastor said something anti-adoption from the pulpit. We never felt closure around those lost relationships and never went back to the church regularly after that Sunday.

These are some ambiguous or disenfranchised losses in Lisa's adoption story as both a first/birth mom and adoptive mom:

- **Loss of my son**—I bonded with him, labored, and birthed him, but for many years, I had no idea where he was, if he was loved and happy, or even if he was alive. Losing him and becoming a first mother was a profound loss. Years later, we were reunited, but the trauma of losing him will always impact me.

- **Loss of privacy as my husband and I pursued adoption**—We found ourselves opening our home and family to so much scrutiny. The home study process can be a bit intrusive, and that was all before the kids came home. Once they were home, we added therapists, physicians, and other professionals, one provider after another.

- **Loss of my family as I knew it**—I had dreamed of how our family would move together through life, and how we would spend holidays, celebrate the big moments, and cling together in the hard times. But that changed after adopting.

- **Loss of sweet sibling relationships**—Over the years, I put a lot of energy into helping my children build close relationships. I imagined a future when they would all be close as adults. After adopting, this dream seemed to evaporate before my eyes.

- **Loss of ease in my marriage**—The amount of stress in my marriage increased with the demands of parenting our children with early trauma. Russ and I were spread so thin that we would have laughed at the idea of a date night. We were no longer free to go out and leave our teens in charge because of challenging behaviors some of our kids exhibited. We missed each other and the relationship we had before adopting. We also had many hard conversations about how to parent our children.

There are six common experiences within the grief process, five originally identified as stages by Swiss-American psychiatrist Elisabeth Kübler-Ross,[3] and then a sixth introduced by death and grieving expert David Kessler.[4] When you grieve, you might move through the stages in a linear fashion, but most often, the process will be more fluid. You may also skip some of the stages. There is no right or wrong way to grieve.

1: Denial

In some ways, denial helps us survive whatever we're going through. This is when everything feels meaningless and overwhelming, and things don't make sense. Sometimes, we might go numb or find ourselves surviving rather than thriving. We may push the feelings away because we must keep going and can't be overwhelmed with fear.

2: Anger or Resentment

As adoptive and foster parents, we often experience anger but struggle because we were the ones who chose the path, even knowing it would be hard. If we're people of faith, it may feel even more complicated—Who are we angry at? Are we angry at God? Are we angry at our spouse for pushing for this decision? Are we angry at the kids because, wow, they're a whole lot harder than we ever imagined? Where does this anger go? When we recognize anger is part of the process, we can accept it, and we don't have to place it on anyone.

3: Bargaining

This is the stage when we ask the "What ifs." "What if I had done something differently?" "What if I had a softer voice?" We may think that if we parent perfectly, learn everything we need to know, or find the best therapist, things will get better. If we're people of faith, we may wonder if things would be better if we were more connected to God. When we're bargaining, we're desperate for something to change our situation.

4: Depression

This is a natural sense of loss. As you begin to realize the truth of your situation, you may feel deeply sad about it. In this part of the grief process, the anger has moved out, and you may feel the weight of the losses. You may have days when you don't think you can go on, and there may be many tears. Sometimes, you may also withdraw because you don't have the energy to be in the midst of lots of people.

5: Acceptance

These losses aren't simple. One day, you'll find yourself pivoting from sadness or anger to a place of acceptance. You didn't expect life to be this way, but you are ready to move forward with the life you have. As a person of faith, you may be ready to tell God, "I'm going to surrender myself to the life and family You've given me." One adoptive parent said it to us like this:

> "I'm not a perfect mom anymore (I realize I never was perfect, but I sure was a lot closer than I am now, and I had a lot of people fooled, especially my children). I miss the Martha Stewart days. The Betty Crocker dinners and rainbows and unicorns. I'm now a Walmart screaming Mom. I miss my fantasy world. I loved the matching outfits and cookie-cutter life. But I absolutely LOVE my new blessing more. I love equally that we DON'T match. Our love is stronger than blood and years of bonding. God fills in our gaps and is even more present in our lives now."

6: Finding Meaning and Purpose

There is something beautiful about helping others as a result of your own struggles. Being able to give back, serve, and redeem some of the hard years brings meaning to the chaos. Parents often feel relieved to look back and know God had a plan and the challenges were not for nothing.

Reflections and Practices for Chapter 2

Day 1: Practice Gratitude

We'll take a deeper dive into gratitude in Chapter 6, but the benefits are so powerful for overcoming shame and guilt that we want you to get started today.

Write down one thing (or more) you're grateful for. Continue adding one thing to this list each day this week.

Day 2: Reflect on Shame

Reflect on your experience of shame in your parenting journey. How did it feel to read quotes from other parents and realize you're not alone?

Day 3: List your Losses

Make a list of your ambiguous or disenfranchised losses.

Day 4: Experience Grief

How are you experiencing grief right now? Consider this list, and circle all that apply:

- Denial
- Anger or resentment
- Bargaining
- Depression
- Acceptance
- Finding meaning and purpose

Take a few moments to process your thoughts by journaling.

Day 5: Read and Reflect

"That God is rich in mercy means that your regions of deepest shame and regret are not hotels through which divine mercy passes but homes in which divine mercy abides. It means the things about you that make you cringe most, make him hug hardest. It means his mercy is not calculating and cautious, like ours. It is unrestrained, flood-like, sweeping, magnanimous. It means our haunting shame is not a problem for him, but the very thing he loves most to work with. It means our sins do not cause his love to take a hit. Our sins cause his love to surge forward all the more. It means on that day when we stand before him, quietly, unhurriedly, we will weep with relief, shocked at how impoverished a view of his mercy-rich heart we had."[5]

PART 2:
The Science of Blocked Trust and Blocked Care

Let's dive a little deeper into the neuroscience behind blocked care. This information holds the key to regaining your compassion.

From the beginning of time, God created humans to be in relationship. As a parent, your nervous system is primed to connect with your children, and the parent-child relationship can foster feelings of deep love and empathy. When you look in your child's eyes and see love reflected back at you, it lights up parts of your brain and seems to go straight to your heart.

Likewise, a child's nervous system is primed to connect with their safe, nurturing caregivers. The child quickly learns that when they cry, a safe adult comes to meet their need. Over and over again, their voice is heard, their need is met, and they experience comfort. They also learn that their behavior can produce happiness in their caregiver.

If the child's needs are not met, and they are neglected or harmed, their nervous system begins to change. This state of chronic distress requires the child to protect themselves. It is so harmful that the child is often unable to receive your attempts of loving connection and care even after being placed in a safe home, no matter how loving and nurturing you are. **This is blocked trust.**

The more you attempt to connect with and care for your child, and the more they appear to resist, it becomes increasingly difficult to keep going. Parents often feel personally rejected, and over time, this results in a sense of feeling angry and sad. It may feel that it's just not worth it anymore because it's too painful. **This is blocked care.** The child's nervous system senses this shift in their parent and feels even more unsafe, which reinforces the parent's sense that the child doesn't want them. And the cycle continues.

In this section, we're going to explain in more depth what is happening in your child's nervous system and in yours. Understanding this will help you regain compassion and find your way back to being the parent you want to be.

Chapter 3:
Understand Blocked Trust

To understand what is going on in your nervous system and how to reclaim compassion, you must go all the way back to what your child experienced before they even came home to you. Adoptees can often face circumstances like the following, all risk factors that would affect their ability to trust:

- prenatal stress or harm
- difficult labor or birth
- early hospitalization
- abuse
- neglect
- trauma
- change in primary caregiver

A child who is exposed to any of these risk factors may subconsciously develop instinctive strategies focused on self-preservation and identifying the next potential threat. This can activate a premature defense mechanism that may put them in a chronic state of survival, resulting in what attachment specialist Dr. Daniel A. Hughes and clinical psychologist Dr. Jonathan Baylin have termed blocked trust.[1]

Because the child is unable to meet their own basic needs and is in chronic distress, their developing brain blocks feelings of hurt and pain in order to tolerate staying near their caregiver. In this state of chronic distress, "the brain uses its pain-relief function—called the analgesic opioid system—to block feelings of hurt or pain in favor of remaining near the adult who can provide these basic necessities."[2]

The child's nervous system is constantly scanning the environment for the next potential threat that may harm them. There is no room to experience feelings of warmth, comfort, kindness, or fun. The pain-relief function activated in their brain also numbs them to feelings of love, joy, affection, and shared happiness.[3]

In a lecture based on his work with Baylin, Hughes identifies these characteristics of blocked trust:

- chronic readiness to defend
- hypervigilance
- reactive emotions (like screaming, that are used to scare people away)
- negativity bias
- inability to notice cues of safety and enjoyment[4]

Even after joining a safe and loving family, these instinctive self-preservation strategies continue. As behaviors, these characteristics may present as lying, stealing, manipulation, bathrooming issues, and food challenges, to name a few.

Your children are survivors, and these skills served them well when they were unsafe and needed to protect themselves from the overwhelming pain of abuse and neglect. But now, these behaviors often lead to the child being labeled as oppositional, controlling, and manipulative. Your child may internalize these labels, which brings shame and leads them to believe they are unworthy and unlovable.

These protective behaviors are automatic responses to fear that may continue even after joining their new family. You know your child is safe now, but your child does not. Here are the experiences of two parents:

> "We have made a lot of progress, but the going is rough most days, and I struggle most with the question of how to like her when she does everything in her power to be unlikeable (hitting, spitting, scratching her older brother; hiding from me; whining about everything)."

> "When my child refused to let me care for him, it led to the unhealthiness of getting really angry that I wasn't being appreciated."

According to Hughes, "[Children in blocked trust] do not have the assumption others will meet their needs. They have to take care of themselves, and they avoid closeness. They keep others at arm's length because getting close is going to lead to abandonment and rejection or abuse. And they see peers, siblings, as competitors. They just don't believe there's enough affection to go around."[5] Your child's nervous system assumes they're in danger and on their own. It develops a confirmation bias that scans for indications that support this assumption. Because of this bias, even neutral situations will be interpreted as negative.

> **Melissa**
> Two of our kids were born to us. They've been surrounded by love and celebration their entire existence, even in utero. They know they are precious, and they are securely attached to us.
>
> One night a couple of summers ago, I forgot to pick one of them up from a friend's house. I could make an excuse about how it was late at night and past my bedtime, but the truth is that it slipped my mind. Because they were secure in their sense of felt safety, they called to remind me, and the ordeal passed without much incident.
>
> On the other hand, four of our kids came to us through adoption. Each has experienced early adversity, resulting in a nervous system that struggles to experience felt safety and is always looking for evidence that relationships *aren't* safe.
>
> During the pandemic, a long-awaited visit with one of our adopted kids had to be canceled due to COVID exposure, which was obviously out of anyone's control. But because of this, their fear center was immediately activated.
>
> "I knew you hated me and didn't want me to visit!" they cried over the phone. "I'm never coming again. I don't need you!"

> It took months for our child to be ready to reengage in a relationship with our family.

We hope learning about blocked trust gives you a clearer picture of what is happening in your child's nervous system and how it hinders their ability to connect with you. Your child is not trying to be difficult—they are simply surviving. And honestly, it's not about you. Any adult who attempted to be their parent would face these same challenges. Knowing this may help you begin reclaiming compassion for your child, which in turn will help you reclaim compassion for yourself.

Reflections and Practices for Chapter 3

Day 1: Practice Lessons in Liking

When we work with parents, they often say this is one of their favorite and most impactful practices. Lisa and her husband Russ developed Lessons in Liking to overcome negative feelings they were experiencing toward one of their children. They desperately wanted to feel warmth toward her, but it was hard.

> **Lisa**
> A little background: Years ago, a wise therapist told Russ and me about a psychological study in which the participants all claimed to hate opera music (hang on—this really is relevant). They were divided into two groups, and both were required to listen to opera music for a certain number of minutes per day. One group simply listened to the assigned opera. The other group listened to the same opera, and then participants wrote their observations of things they liked about it. The first day, they recorded one thing they liked. The second day, they wrote down two things they liked. The third, three, and so on. At the end of the experiment, the group that had not recorded its observations still proclaimed to hate opera, while the second group had developed more of a taste for it.
>
> Though I tried, I never was able to confirm the details of the study, but I always found the concept fascinating, especially given our experience with adoption. The study implies that when people look beyond the obvious challenges with something and push themselves to seek

> something they like about it, they begin to find it more likable. Something changes in their minds and alters the way they see it.
>
> Russ and I took the idea of the opera study and applied it to our relationship with our daughter. We called this simple practice "Lessons in Liking." For several weeks, we texted each other daily with one thing we liked about this child. Sometimes, it was quick and easy, and other times, we struggled to think of something to say. But we kept at it.
>
> This exercise wound up having a profound impact in the way I felt about my daughter. As my mind focused on the likable qualities of my child, I found her more likable. I saw the sweetness, the sparkly eyes, the lively personality, and I could appreciate her. When I looked past the struggles to see the good, some healing happened in my heart, and I could relate to her in a calmer way. As this change happened in me, my daughter began to feel safer and more secure with me.

Every child needs to be delighted over, but many of our children missed this in their early childhood. Perhaps they spent those years in an orphanage or with a dying parent. Perhaps they were neglected or abused. These wounded children may have challenging behaviors clouding their ability to see or believe the truth—that they are beloved, made in the image of God. He delights over them, and so should we, even if it takes a bit of practice.

Your simple practice this week is to commit to exchanging texts about a likeable quality of your child with your spouse, a friend, or another person who cares for you and your child. We had a dad write to us once who said, "I just read this and thought, 'Ugh! I do NOT want to do this.' Guess that means I need to. I'm in!" We encourage you to give this practice a try. The results could be life changing.

Day 2: Identify Risk Factors

Do any of these risk factors apply to your child? Even one is enough to change the way their nervous system interprets the world.

- prenatal stress or harm
- difficult labor or birth
- early hospitalization or medical trauma
- abuse
- neglect
- toxic stress
- change in primary caregiver

Today, think about how your child's current behavior may be influenced by their earliest experiences. Making connections between their past and their behavior may help you develop greater compassion for them.

Day 3: Notice Confirmation Bias

Reflect on the story Melissa shared about her two kids. Does your child have a confirmation bias of safety? Or does your child have a confirmation bias of danger? How do you see this reflected in the way your child reacts?

Day 4: Reflect on Lessons in Liking

Together, with your Lessons in Liking partner, create a list of things you have shared that you like about your child. Continue adding to this list for the next few weeks. Then, save it for the days when you need a reminder.

Day 5: Read and Reflect

> "This I call to mind, and therefore I have hope:
> The steadfast love of the Lord never ceases; his mercies never come to an end"
> (Lam. 3:21–22 ESV).

What do you need to call to mind? When has the Lord shown mercy to you? Reflect back over your life, asking the Holy Spirit to bring experiences to your mind. Write a few down and reflect on them.

Chapter 4: Understand Blocked Care

This chapter is packed with information about blocked care. That means there is a lot of neuroscience for you to soak in. As you read and learn, be kind to yourself; don't be ashamed of your feelings because it's normal and okay to feel them. Blocked care is difficult, and the fact that you're even experiencing it shows that your nervous system is working as it's supposed to. That's something to be thankful about.

In order to understand how to overcome blocked care and reconnect with your child, you need to understand how your brain is primed to provide compassionate care for your child and be responsive to their needs.

As a parent, you are wired to initiate interactions with your child. This could be a smile, affectionate touch, or a simple, "Good morning." Your nervous system is expecting a positive response in return. Even a small nod would encourage you to keep approaching your child for connection.

This cycle of positive interactions keeps your nervous system open to the relationship. In this open state, you're able to stay curious about your child's behavior and have empathy for their experiences. For example, when your child comes home from school, throws their backpack on the floor, and collapses on the sofa, you may think, "My child must be really tried," or "Something didn't go well at school today." Instead of asking them to hang up their backpack, you flop down next to them and say, "It looks like you had a long day at school. Do you want me to get you a snack while you tell me about it?"

However, if your attempts at connection are met with stony silence or even rejection, your nervous system may retreat as blocked care sets in. When your child consistently doesn't respond to your efforts of caregiving and connection, you may begin to feel ineffective and experience a sense of failure. This lack of reciprocity in the relationship feels confusing and may remind your nervous system of past rejections or abandonments. Your nervous system's defensive reaction to your child's self-protective rejection is likely to grow stronger and reduce your capacity for empathy. You may stop being motivated to engage your child.

In this self-protective mode, managing complex thinking becomes difficult, which hinders your ability to see the need behind your child's behavior. You may take challenging behaviors personally or assume your child is doing them on purpose.

Thankfully, even in blocked care, you are still purposefully caring for your child's needs, regardless of how your child responds to you. You get up each morning to feed your kids. You do laundry, so they have clean clothes. You consistently take care of their basic needs, regardless of how you feel on a given day.

We share this to help you make sense of why you feel and respond the way you do.

When your brain is parenting at its best, you can stay present and attuned enough to enhance your child's brain development and build strong bonds of trust.[1] In contrast, when you're experiencing blocked care many of your caregiving instincts are, at least temporarily, suppressed.[2] You're still going through all the motions of providing practical care for your children, but your heart is no longer in it.

Your brain knows you're making efforts to connect with your child, but lack of response, or even a negative response from your child, is confusing. Over time, the nervous system begins to protect you from what it perceives as impending danger.

When this happens, a sense of "I don't recognize myself," often sets in. You may find yourself being harsh or indifferent toward your child and, at the same time, thinking, "What is wrong with me?"

Ten Signs of Blocked Care

In our work, we observed many signs of blocked care, which led us to develop a list of ten specific signs parents and professionals should be aware of. You may remember these signs from the pre-reading assessment at the beginning of the book and recognize that your experience with them can range anywhere from a lot to a little.

If you're experiencing even one of these signs, know that you're not alone. Thousands of parents are with you on this hard journey. Take a look at the signs and what parents have to say:

1. You are too caught up in coping with your child's behavior to be curious about the meaning behind it.

> "Our son, who was adopted as an older child, has been very challenging. He can charm everyone he meets but saves his defiance and manipulative behaviors especially for me. It hurts. It is fatiguing. It is trying. I'm too tired to figure it out."

2. You feel defensive and guard yourself from rejection.

> "When he is acting out, and I am at my worst, I can hardly be in the same room with him. It is not fair to him, and it is absolutely a sole reflection of my inadequacies—not his. But I don't know how to repair it. I never thought I would be in this position. How could anyone not like a child?"

3. You feel burned out, chronically overwhelmed, and fatigued.

> "I'm failing as a mom and as a Christian to these kids put in my care. I am tired of the crazy controlling fighting, unthankful begging, nonstop eating, won't-give-me-5-seconds-to-myself life

right now. I have said things I should not say after he kicks and hits and fights and hurts people for no reason. Help."

"I feel like my blood pressure must be going through the roof because even when my words are patient and I have a smile on my face, I am about to boil over. Mostly, I wonder—will it get better? I used to be so happy and at peace with my family. I used to be so happy with myself as a mother. I want it back."

"I work in the medical field. I'm not able to work full time because my brain can't handle it. I'm worried I will inadvertently harm someone. I've had to give up part of my career and start on antidepressants. It is so tough feeling incompetent."

4. You feel resentment toward one or more of your children or your situation as a whole. You may even regret adopting or fostering.

"I have a hard time enjoying parenting. I feel resentful when I have to adjust my plans due to their mistakes, behaviors, or needs."

"My husband and I are on the brink of losing our minds. Our once very strong marriage has been suffering. We both feel such regret and somewhat resentment toward each other about our decision to adopt."

5. You feel irritable with other family and friends.

"On the outside (to others), she appears as this darling sweet little thing. But they don't live with us. They don't live with the lying, manipulating, nonstop talking, bossiness, etc. I am starting to show physical signs of stress. This is eating me alive. I was once an organized, fun, happy mom. Now I'm irritable, depressed, and anxious. I'm not sure what to do. I'm praying God will change my heart soon. I find some comfort in knowing I'm not alone."

6. You isolate yourself.

"I felt I couldn't tell anyone what was happening in our family—who would believe a 5 ½-year-old could really wreak havoc the way she could? I wanted to hide and besides, I had no energy to even think about being around other people."

7. You become cynical about helpful ideas.

"Do you honestly think anything will help? It feels like we're throwing money at one thing after another. I just want to feel normal, but I don't know if I'll ever feel it again."

8. You feel you've lost compassion, which leads to shame.

"I once was a happy mom who woke up and wanted to make Mickey Mouse pancakes. Now, I find myself asking the kids to wait one more minute (which turns into longer), so I can try to convince myself to get up and be happy. I grieve for my old life, and I know this is selfish. Most of my time and energy and thoughts are consumed by how I can make this all work."

"My husband feels so much shame about disliking a child, but we feel almost resentment for our son because it's always about him. It's a really hard place for us, and we literally get on our knees and pray."

9. You experience a crisis of faith or challenge of a personal belief system.

> "We thought we were being faithful Christians and following God's instruction to care for orphans. It feels like our obedience has led to one crisis after another and our family is falling apart. Where is God now?"

> "I rest some days now in where I am, yet the angst inevitably returns. Aching to like, feel something more positive than I do, be released to love as I was designed to love. But nothing helps—I've lost hope."

10. You don't feel real pleasure in parenting.

> "One thing is a bit scary to me. Because of all the really difficult years of numbing myself to the abuse in order to function as a parent, I still feel a bit numb. I don't get as excited about things as I used to. I'm more cynical and less confident. I don't even know if I'm capable of feeling love like I used to. But I can show it. And I guess I'll just have to keep asking God to help my feelings follow my actions. Only He can heal my hurt heart. Only He can heal my kids' hurt hearts. We have that in common."

You picked up this book to find a way to overcome blocked care and develop compassion, so you can have a loving relationship with your child. With a better understanding of the connection between neuroscience and what you see in the day-to-day interactions with your child, you'll be able to work more effectively through blocked care by yourself and with your spouse or another support person. One mom contacted us to say,

> "Learning about blocked care helped me talk to my husband about what I have been feeling and be open with him. Also hearing from him that he is feeling much the same—and here I thought he was just feeling so in love with her and enjoying her. Not that I wish these feelings on him, but we can now work through this together."

A huge part of feeling and doing better is knowing you're not alone and having someone validate your feelings. We hope that through the stories and experiences of other parents in this book, including us, you'll gain the knowledge you need to reclaim the compassion you want to feel for your child.

Types of Blocked Care

Once again, it's important to emphasize that blocked care is not something that happens consciously. Your nervous system is protecting you without your permission. This is not a character flaw. After repeated rejection or long periods of disconnection, your heart may lose its tenderness toward your child. Sometimes, you may fear your child or find it hard to even be in the same room.

While a lot of blocked care is in response to a child having blocked trust, in *Brain-Based Parenting*, Hughes and Baylin list four different types of blocked care.[3] This is how we describe them.

Acute Blocked Care

This happens during an acute period of stress, which overwhelms a parent's nervous system. Examples might be clinical depression, an unexpected job loss, divorce, or even a natural disaster, like living near a wildfire in California. The parent is so overwhelmed that their normal caregiving responses become temporarily blocked.

Child-Specific Blocked Care

This happens when a specific child has difficulties with connecting, due to early childhood trauma or neurodiversity. If you have a child who is aggressive toward you or toward a more vulnerable child in your family, it's difficult to remain open to connection. Child-specific blocked care may also occur if a child reminds the parent of someone in their past with whom they had a difficult relationship. One parent told us,

> "I have so much shame about the way I feel toward one of my five kids. I hate that it's just one kid, and it feels like something is wrong with me that I can't be the 'bigger person' and stop feeling this way (it's not like my other four are perfect, but I don't have the same negative bias toward them that I do toward the one). It helped to learn that my brain did this to protect me, and that makes me feel a little less at fault. Hopeful that this will help me take little steps to get back to the mom I used to love being."

Stage-Specific Blocked Care

This happens when behaviors from a specific stage of child development are difficult for a parent to receive. You may be familiar with the argumentative stage kids seem to hit in their early teens. Some parents can roll with it, while others find it extremely difficult. This can lead to a parent beginning to shut down toward connection with their child.

Chronic Blocked Care

This happens when a parent's caregiving system is poorly developed due to experiencing early adversity or toxic stress in childhood without the support of a caring adult. The brain areas needed for a healthy parental response are underdeveloped, making it almost impossible for the parent to nurture the child appropriately without first receiving significant healing and support.

As you can see, not all types of blocked care are the result of parenting a child in blocked trust. We work with parents experiencing all four of these types of blocked care. However, child-specific blocked care related to blocked trust is the type we commonly observe in adoptive and foster parents.

If this is your circumstance, we hope this information helps you understand that blocked care is your nervous system's way of protecting you from the painful and confusing challenge of parenting a child in blocked trust. If you are experiencing one of the other types of blocked care, there are many reasons your nervous system is protecting you as well.

We'll say it again: you are not a bad parent. There is hope! The nervous system can heal and as it does, your heart will regain compassion once again.

Reflections and Practices for Chapter 4

Day 1: Speak Truth

Surround yourself with words of truth. Find a positive affirmation, quote, or scripture that speaks life to you. Write it on a sticky note and put it somewhere where you'll see it multiple times each day.

Here are some examples we've seen from other parents:

"A bad day doesn't make me a bad parent."

"I am doing more good than I know."

"'The LORD is close to the brokenhearted and saves those who are crushed in spirit' (Ps. 34:18 NIV)."

"I can do hard things."

"Just keep swimming!"

"'The LORD your God is with you. He is mighty to save' (Zeph. 3:17 ESV)."

"I am not alone."

"My hope is found in Christ."

"I am deeply loved."

"God's grace is sufficient for you and His power is made perfect in weakness! (2 Cor. 12:9)."

"'My help comes from the LORD, the Maker of heaven and earth' (Psalm 121:2 NIV)."

"I am A PARENTING SUPERSTAR!"

"Brokenness will not have the last word."

"This too shall pass."

"Relationships with my children can be repaired and restored. Don't give up!"

"You don't reap the harvest the day you plant the seed."

"'The steadfast love of the LORD never ceases; his mercies never come to an end; they are new every morning; great is your faithfulness' (Lam. 3:22-23 ESV)."

"Just breathe."

And here's our personal favorite that we say at the close of every podcast episode:

"You're a good parent doing good work."

Day 2: Signs of Blocked Care

How many signs of blocked care are you experiencing? How severe do they seem? Are you surprised by any of the signs listed?

- I'm too caught up in coping with my child's behavior to be curious about the meaning behind it.
- I feel defensive and guard myself from rejection.
- I feel burned out, chronically overwhelmed, and fatigued.
- I feel resentment toward one or more of my children or my situation as a whole. I may even regret adopting or fostering.
- I feel irritable with other family and friends.
- I isolate myself.
- I'm cynical about helpful ideas.
- I've lost compassion, which has led to shame.
- I've experienced a crisis of faith or challenge of a personal belief system.
- I don't feel real pleasure in parenting.

Day 3: Caring for Your Child

Which parts of parenting feel hard right now? Which parts are easier for you to do?

- Initiating connection with your child
- Noticing and empathizing with your child's emotional state
- Staying curious about the meaning behind your child's behaviors
- Meeting your child's basic needs

Day 4: Types of Blocked Care

What type(s) of blocked care are you experiencing?

- Acute blocked care
- Child-specific blocked care
- Stage-specific blocked care
- Chronic blocked care

Day 5: Read and Reflect

"Dear Child of God, I write these words because we all experience sadness, we all come at times to despair, and we all lose hope that the suffering in our lives and in the world will ever end. I want to share with you my faith and my understanding that this suffering can be transformed and redeemed. There is no such thing as a totally hopeless case. Our God is an expert at dealing with chaos, with brokenness, with all the worst that we can imagine. God created order out of disorder, cosmos out of chaos, and God can do so always, can do so now—in our personal lives and in our lives as nations, globally. . . . Indeed, God is transforming the world now—through us—because God loves us."[4]

PART 3: The Process of Overcoming Blocked Care

As mentioned before, your brain is primed to connect with your children and have empathy for their emotional experience. However, children with blocked trust suppress feelings of sadness and hurt, and instead, display behaviors that push people away. Their nervous systems are protecting them from potential danger. Empathy will probably not be your first reaction to their challenging behaviors. The challenge is for you to choose radical compassion.[1] This requires you to use your higher-level thinking instead of reacting instinctively. Reclaiming compassion includes actively remembering your child's past and how it is influencing their current behavior, which will lead you to empathy.

In order to act intentionally instead of instinctively, you need a sense of felt safety. Felt safety isn't a conscious knowledge. Every second, your nervous system is subconsciously processing millions of stimuli from your body, your environment, and other nervous systems close by. Based on your history, your nervous system filters all of that data to perceive if you're safe or in danger, then signals your body to respond accordingly. This process is called neuroception.

If your nervous system senses stress or danger, it will either activate or collapse to increase your chances of survival. Activation can be fighting the threat or attempting to physically remove yourself from the situation. When the nervous system is extremely overwhelmed, it may collapse, going numb and dissociating. Sometimes, it moves quickly between these states or uses a combination, whatever it instinctively senses will give you the best chance of survival.

Chronic stress has negative effects on your mind and body, particularly if you feel helpless to change your circumstances. If you can't see your way out of the situation despite your best efforts, you may become worried or depressed and lose your sense of felt safety.

Brain imaging has shown that the emotional experience of being rejected activates the same pattern in the brain as physical pain. The two are processed in the same way. When a parent approaches a child anticipating positive reactions and instead gets a negative response, it activates the social rejection system. You might then respond to this rejection in the same way you would respond to physical pain—by drawing away and protecting yourself. It is literally painful.

You may also viscerally feel this in your stomach or chest. The gut reaction you have to your children's rejection is likely to grow stronger and reduce your capacity for empathy, unless you are aware it's happening and intentionally care for your nervous system to keep your empathy and compassion from running out.

To sustain empathetic parenting, you must have felt safety when you interact with your child. The challenge is to stay in "safe mode," even when your child is *not* in their "safe mode." If you can stay regulated and in charge of your nervous system, even when your child shifts to a protective stress response, you are much more likely to access radical compassion and respond in a caring, helpful way. This fosters their emotional intelligence, strengthens their ability to regulate, and invites them to show their more vulnerable feelings.

This is why your own nervous system health is so vital to creating a positive cycle of care. We know this may seem like an insurmountable goal, but you can start with small steps, such as the simple practices at the end of each chapter.

Nervous System Care

You need consistent and intentional nervous system care to reduce stress, increase your capacity, and stay motivated to offer compassionate care to your child. Your vagus nerve, which is in charge of your neuroception, is bi-directional. This means your subconscious sense of neuroception can set off a cascade of physical effects in your body, like increasing your heart rate. But it also means if you decrease your heart rate through deep breathing, you can cue to your neuroception that you're okay. By providing consistent cues of safety to your nervous system, you're empowering it to stay in "safe mode." This enables your nervous system to feel safe even if your child is unable to engage in a reciprocal relationship.

We encourage you to think about nervous system care by making sure you're filling up three buckets:

1. **Internal World**—includes things you do for your physical well-being and to maintain a healthy mindset
2. **External World**—how you set up your environment and meet your sensory needs
3. **Relational World**—making sure you have a foundational relationship with God and fulfilling relationships with other safe people, so you can pour into your kids

Habits

In the upcoming chapters, we're going to share several simple practices to help you overcome blocked care. We know your life is full, and this may seem overwhelming, but we know the trick is incorporating these practices into your life by creating new habits.

To help you accomplish this, here are some of our best tips, including some of our favorites from James Clear's fabulous book, *Atomic Habits*:[2]

Habit Stack

One of the best ways to build a new habit is to identify a current habit you've already established and stack your new behavior on top of it.[3] For example, if you want to begin reading 15 minutes a day, look for a habit you already have. If you eat breakfast every morning, try reading for 15 minutes while you eat. You'll be more likely to create the habit of reading because you've attached it to a habit you already have.

Set Up Your Environment for Success

You'll be more likely to go to the gym in the morning if you set out your clothes and water bottle the night before. You'll be more successful establishing a routine of reading your Bible if you keep your Bible next to your favorite chair.

Pair Something You Need with Something You Want

If you need to create a consistent habit of walking on a treadmill, choose a favorite television show and only allow yourself to watch it once you're moving.

Find an Accountability Partner

A partner can increase your probability of establishing a new habit in amazing ways. If you know your friend is picking you up at 5:30 AM to go to the gym, you're much more likely to be up and ready than if you are going on your own.

Take Tiny Steps

Kaizen is a Japanese term meaning "change for the better" or "continuous improvement." It may seem ridiculous, but if you want to establish a habit of doing yoga, do one downward dog each day. If you need more sleep, go to bed five minutes earlier each night (pro tip: put on your pajamas while you help your kids get ready for bed). Tiny, incremental steps lead to significant change over time.

Chapter 5:
Be Kind to Your Body

Remember that to begin overcoming blocked care, you need to learn to cue safety to your nervous system through three types of habits: taking care of your internal, external, and relational worlds. This week, you'll begin filling your internal world bucket by being kind to your body. This chapter provides you with practical and essential ways to do that.

Improve Your Sleep

We all know it's important to get enough sleep for our health and well-being, yet many people struggle to sleep enough. They read about sleep, talk to doctors, take supplements or medication, and even monitor their sleep with phone apps, but getting the true rest they need at night can be a challenge. The thing is, it's hard to be a great parent when you're exhausted. In this section, we'll share with you some of our best tips for better sleep.

Establish a Bedtime Routine

We recommend beginning to prepare for a good night of sleep after dinner. Tidy the house, and set out anything you need for the morning. Be selective about how you spend your evening hours. If there is a show you plan to watch, ask yourself honestly if there is enough time to finish it before your planned bedtime, or if it's likely to cause you to stay up too late. Reading or listening to a book may be more conducive to going to bed on time.

Blocking blue light from screens can help your brain calm. Many phones have a "night shift" setting, which changes the phone display to warmer tones. You can also purchase special glasses to wear in the evening that block blue light.

Consider setting an alarm to remind you when it's time to head to bed. Lisa's favorite is the sound of crickets that goes off at 9:00 PM each night; it prompts her to wrap up what she's doing and go to bed.

Minimize Noise

Those of us who struggle with sleep know how easy it is to be woken by noise. Whether it's an older kid coming home late or a loud neighbor, noise disturbs sleep. Two things make a big difference. First, consider buying a sound machine, and turn it on each night as you get ready for bed; not only will it help block out noise, but you'll begin to associate the sound it makes with going to sleep. Second, if you don't have little ones who may need care during the night, sleep with soft earplugs to block out even more noise.

Drink More Water

With so much crazy in our lives, we sometimes neglect to do the basics our body needs, like drinking water. Water makes up more than half of our body and plays a crucial role in every critical bodily function. It's necessary for joint, skin, and digestive health, and helps our body cleanse itself of dangerous toxins.[1] Conversely, even mild dehydration can cause headaches, impair energy levels and mood, and lead to major reductions in memory and brain performance.[2]

Ideally, you should be drinking at least half your body weight in ounces of water each day. For example, if you're 140 pounds, you should drink 70 ounces of water.[3] We know what you're thinking: "I'll be running to the bathroom all day long!" And we hear you. But think of all the quick breaks you'll get from your kids! Plus, one of the quickest ways to regulate your nervous system is to relax your pelvic floor, which naturally happens when you urinate.[4] Basically, drinking more water will make you pee more, which will keep you more regulated.

It's important to note that sweetened and caffeinated drinks will not keep you hydrated in the way you need. In some cases, they dehydrate you more quickly.

On the flip side, adding a couple of drops of an essential oil high in limonene to your water can reduce stress.[5] Essential oils high in d-limonene are lemon, lime, wild orange, and grapefruit. Be sure to use an essential oil rated for internal use.

And if you're someone who has always had a hard time with wanting to drink water, try this tip from a fellow parent:

> "Drinking with a straw makes all the difference for me. I use a mason jar with a straw and keep it on the counter near the entrance to our kitchen, which I pass by all the time."

Move More

We all know movement and exercise are important for physical health. It's also good for your emotional and mental state. When you get your heart rate up, your body releases feel-good endorphins that reduce stress. In her book, *The Joy of Movement*, Kelly McGonigal writes about the science behind "hope molecules"—chemicals released by the muscles into the bloodstream during exercise to protect the brain from stress. "These chemicals can [actually] help people recover from trauma," she says. "Every time you move, you are giving yourself an intravenous dose of hope."[6]

If you're not a regular exerciser, start small. Do ten jumping jacks before each meal. Or if your kids are already running around in the backyard, join them. You may also want to try yoga; there are many free videos online, so you don't even have to leave your home to attend a class.

You can also simply begin walking. Walking is incredibly beneficial and can be done at any pace for any length of time. Being in nature is good for your nervous system, but a treadmill on a winter day is just fine too.

One parent had this piece of advice to share:

"My favorite way to exercise is to walk with a friend! Gets me moving and connecting. I used to meet friends over coffee, but I've tried to switch that to walks as often as possible."

Improve Your Nutrition

Nutrition is the foundation of every process in a person's body. If you're experiencing brain fog, fatigue, hair loss, or more, focusing on nutrition could be a key. Part of being kind to your body means that you pay attention to which foods energize you or make you feel sluggish. Maybe one cup of coffee helps you wake up in the morning but three makes you anxious and jittery. Be mindful also of your body's need for high-quality food. You need to have balance and energy to meet the intense demands of your family, especially if you're going through challenging times.

Stay on Top of Your Health

Finally, take care of routine medical and dental care and any other aspects of your health. And, by all means, give yourself permission to rest if you're sick or injured. We know you probably feel like you can't afford the time, the effort, or the cost, but we've heard from far too many parents who neglected to care for themselves as they worked hard to meet the needs of everyone else, and who made things harder for themselves as a result. Often they didn't realize how awful they felt, and small manageable problems became bigger and more serious.

Lisa

As Russ and I were packing to leave for Ethiopia to bring our daughter home, I realized it hurt to chew on

> one side of my mouth. Something felt a little irritated and sore. No big deal, I figured, thinking it would get better on its own. But while out of the country, the vague pain I felt began to focus on one tooth, so I was careful not to put pressure on it, telling myself I'd figure it out later.
>
> We got home, and the pace of life was so intense that I couldn't think about myself or any of my needs. Yet the pain in my tooth didn't go away and in fact felt worse. After finally scheduling an appointment and getting X-rays, the dentist told me the tooth was infected and had to be pulled. I remember being stunned because I'd never had a serious dental problem before, and now my molar had to come out? You can imagine how much I wished I'd taken care of it when it was a small problem.

As you take good care of your body, you will have more energy and strength for the effort required to continue the process of overcoming blocked care. Remember: this is a marathon, not a sprint.

Reflections and Practices for Chapter 5

Day 1: Tune in to Your Body

Find a comfortable position, whether sitting or lying down. Inhale deeply, taking a breath that expands down into your belly. Fully exhale, contracting your belly to push all the air out of your body. Slowly scan your body from head to toe. Do you notice any tightness, discomfort, or other sensations? Maybe you even notice that you're hungry or thirsty. Relax your jaw and soften your tongue. Notice how your body relaxes. Take one more deep breath with an extended exhale before you return to whatever parenting duties await.

Day 2: Improve Your Sleep

What are your sleep challenges? Write your thoughts below.

Choose one thing that will improve your sleep and try it for several days. Consider adding more sleep supports over the next several weeks.

What will you try first? How about second?

Day 3: Drink More Water

Fill up your favorite water bottle and drink more water today. If you don't have a water bottle you love, look for one that has the right feel or is a color that makes you happy. Try adding a few drops of lemon essential oil to your water each morning.

Day 4: Move Your Body

Take a short walk or spend five minutes stretching. How did it feel while you were doing it? How do you feel now?

Day 5: Read and Reflect

"The body is physically restricted when emotions are bound up inside. People's shoulders tighten; their facial muscles tense. They spend enormous amounts of energy on holding back their tears—or any sound or movement that might betray their inner state. When the physical tension is released, the feelings can be released."[7]

Chapter 6: Establish a Healthy Mindset

This week, we're continuing to focus on filling your internal world bucket by working toward a healthy mindset. In order to reclaim compassion for yourself and your kids, it's imperative to fill your mind with truth and correct the narratives that keep you from wanting to connect with your kids.

The apostle Paul offers a great example of the importance of choosing where we focus our minds. In Philippians 4:4–7 (NIV), he says,

> "Rejoice in the Lord always. I will say it again: Rejoice! Let your gentleness be evident to all. The Lord is near. Do not be anxious about anything, but in every situation, by prayer and petition, with thanksgiving, present your requests to God. And the peace of God, which transcends all understanding, will guard your hearts and your minds in Christ Jesus."

When Paul says we should present our prayers with thanksgiving, maybe it's as simple as saying, "Thank you, Lord. I'm giving this to you now." The peace of God is available to us. We need to take every situation, by prayer and petition, with thanksgiving, to the Lord. Paul then continues in Philippians 4:8 (NIV),

> "Finally, brothers and sisters, whatever is true, whatever is noble, whatever is right, whatever is pure, whatever is lovely, whatever is admirable—if anything is excellent or praiseworthy—think about such things."

The Bible tells us to meditate on good things. This requires discipline and a willingness to change our thoughts. To establish a healthy mindset, we encourage you to surround yourself with things that remind you to focus on the good in your life.

Definition of Success

It's easy to fall into the trap of defining successful parenting by factors that are ultimately out of our control. Many parents are looking for improved behavior or for their kids to be contributing members of society.

Here are some definitions of success parents have shared with us:

> "Our kids will feel connected and loved."

> "I have seen success as no meltdowns, good attitudes, and obedience."

"Have my kiddo in independent living."

"My child will love the Lord."

"A peaceful home."

Unfortunately, even the seemingly low bar of "My kid won't end up in prison," is out of our control and not always realistic.

As it turns out, you can't control how your kids feel about being in your family, how they do academically, or who they choose as friends. Even with the best connected-parenting tools, you can't control their behavior. This doesn't make you a failure.

But what you can control is yourself. If you define success around your kids' reactions or behaviors, you are setting yourself up to fail. We encourage you to define success by factors you can control, for example:

- Our children will be heard, and their feelings accepted.
- We will model regulation and repair.
- We will provide a safe place until our kids are ready to launch. We believe they will when they can.
- We will model God's love and kindness.
- I will get enough sleep each night, so I have the energy to co-regulate the kids.
- We will provide a safe place for our kids to come back to, regardless of the size of the failure.

Additionally, you can attend support groups to have the encouragement to keep putting your heart out to your kids.

You can pray, go to your own therapy appointments, and do your best to be the adult, even in the hardest of situations.

Since we've chosen to define success by our actions and not the reactions of our kids, we've seen the shame of failure melting away. We want this for each one of you too.

The key to overcoming blocked care and regaining compassion for your child is experiencing what your child also needs—nurture and felt safety.

How do you currently define success as a parent? Is it something you have control over? If not, what will your new definition of success be?

Negativity Bias

When you're in blocked care, you are easily overcome by negativity bias. All humans have this negativity bias. It's why we're more affected by criticism than compliments. When you're not experiencing chronic stress, this is an effective self-protective mechanism because it alerts you to danger.

Your nervous system reacts to things based on connections between neurons in the brain that send signals from one part of your brain to another. These are called neural pathways. Think of them like ruts in a dirt road. The more you drive on those worn paths, the deeper the ruts get. Similarly, the more you connect two things in your brain, the stronger the neural pathway becomes.

You can interrupt your typical pattern of negativity—the chain reaction of neural pathways—with an unexpected moment of fun or gratitude. When you find yourself being pulled down by negativity, do something intentional to break out of the rut. This is called a pattern interrupt.

You may be experiencing daily extreme stress as you parent children with significant needs, and you may feel negativity bias is coloring everything happening between you and your child.

> **Lisa**
> My daughter had many food issues due to chronic malnourishment and intentional deprivation of food in her past. One of the effects was a strong desire for her to control her food. The upside to this was that she loved cooking. The downside was that she was a very messy cook, and she generally refused to share with her siblings, even when she'd made a large quantity of food.
>
> One afternoon, after being gone for an appointment, I walked into the kitchen to find a mess. Oil and spices were spilled on the counters, and the stove was covered with rice. I could feel frustration and anger rising; in that moment, I thought this was just one more mess, one more time my daughter had taken advantage of my absence. But then I glanced into the dining room where the table was set for dinner. My daughter, together with her younger sister, ran out of the room, saying, "Surprise! We cooked dinner!"
>
> My negativity bias could have caused me to react in anger, but the short pause between my initial thought

> and the girls revealing their surprise allowed me to see more clearly.
>
> The power of the pause—the gap of time between my initial thought and my response—was exactly what I needed to pull myself out of the rut in my thoughts and into a new place of hope.

> **Melissa**
> One of our kids talks nonstop. Anybody else? Our entire family has succumbed to negativity bias regarding our son's voice. Now, even if he talks at an appropriate time, we have this urge to tell him to "Be quiet!"

Part of overcoming blocked care is recognizing your tendency toward negativity and pausing to consider what might actually be happening. It's imperative to take a moment and consider the possibility that this may not be the same old behavior from the same kid.

You need to put effort into truly valuing all the good and positive aspects of your life to avoid being overcome by the negative. Even if you are facing a multitude of objectively negative situations, you can try to appreciate the positive aspects of your life, regardless of how small they may be.

Practice Gratitude

If you are a person of faith, you have a compelling reason to practice gratitude—God tells you to be thankful. You may be struggling, weary, scared, or even wondering where God is in this trial. But He is steadfast, always loving you, never leaving you.

You can choose to have a heart of thanksgiving, and when you don't have the strength to make the conscious choice, ask God to give it to you. You can't always change what is happening around you, but you can ask Him to change your heart.

Pastor and author Max Lucado teaches, "A heart cannot be grateful and anxious at the same time. When gratitude walks in, anxiety walks out. Anxiety focuses on what we don't have or are about to lose. Gratitude focuses on what God has done."[1] Gratitude gets your eyes off yourself and your circumstances. It reminds you that you are not in control and are utterly dependent on God. He is your provider and giver of all good gifts.

God's Word is filled with many reminders of how powerful and vital a thankful heart can be in this world. Colossians 2:6–7 (CSB) tells us,

> ". . . just as you received Christ Jesus as Lord, continue to walk in him, being rooted and built up in him and established in the faith, just as you were taught, and overflowing with gratitude."

Gratitude is not just a good idea, it's good for your brain. When practiced regularly, gratitude produces feelings of long-lasting happiness and contentment. This happens because your brain releases dopamine and serotonin, the two crucial neurotransmitters responsible for positive emotions.

By consciously practicing gratitude every day, you strengthen the neural pathways, those connections in your brain, and gratitude becomes more of who you are and how you move through the world. It helps you see the positive and accept your present situation, even when it's hard.

Gratitude is also good for your physical health. Research shows that participants who kept an online gratitude journal for two weeks reported better physical health, including fewer headaches, less stomach pain, clearer skin, and reduced congestion.[2]

Gratitude helps you sustain relationships and appreciate people. And guess what? Gratitude increases empathy.

Here are some practical ways to practice gratitude:

Gratitude Journal

Record things you are grateful for in a simple journal. We recommend committing to a daily practice of adding at least one entry each day. Use a bound journal, a school notebook, or even the Notes feature on your phone. Most of all, just get started. If you're a morning person, reflect on the previous day. If you're more of a night owl, reflect before bed. And once each week, look back at previous entries to remind yourself of the many gifts in your life.

Gratitude App

There are several free apps for recording and tracking gratitude. Set a reminder that pops up each day to help you be consistent.

Sticky Notes

If you are a visual person who wants to record thoughts of gratitude on the fly, use simple sticky notes. Write a quick note and stick it on the wall near you. Lisa likes to put them above her kitchen sink. Katie Davis, the author of *Daring to Hope*, covered her kitchen wall with gratitude sticky notes.[3]

Keep a Family Gratitude Jar

Keep a glass jar and a stack of small pieces of paper beside it in your kitchen or dining room. Each day, write one thing you are grateful for. It can be very simple. As your jar fills up, you'll have a visual reminder of the blessings in your life.

Laugh More

When parenting in stressful circumstances, humor is often the first thing to go. Who has time for play when the goal is behavior modification? You want obedience. You want compliance. Traditional parenting tells you to withhold fun to "convince" a child he should obey. This can be the start of a terrible downward spiral because playfulness is one of the most effective ways of deescalating challenging behaviors and keeping your kids moving in the right direction.

Playfulness and fun keep your nervous system open for connection, these parents agree:

> "The other day, my son was starting to get frustrated. I wanted to avoid a meltdown and remembered this lesson. I said, 'Come and look at the biggest fart ever!' He loved the YouTube video of the hippo fart. We went on to watch funny animal videos, and he

laughed so much. He has been in a decent mood since! Thank you so much for this tip!"

"My kids think the Minions are hilarious, so I found a compilation of short Minion clips. I was surprised at how well these clips worked as a motivator for them to finish cleaning their rooms and eat breakfast when I said we'd do a fun activity after 'if there was time.' At first, my oldest didn't want to participate, but he soon plopped down on my other side. Both kids sat next to me on the couch and giggled about bananas. My youngest even asked if we can do it again tomorrow."

"We didn't watch a video, but I did look up silly kids' jokes, and then I spelled out the question of the joke with my finger on his back. He's super ticklish and laughed the whole time. He wrote each letter on a tablet; then read it to me. When he read the joke question, I responded with the punchline. Then, we flipped roles. I like play with purpose. I like that we laughed, had physical touch, and practiced spelling and reading. It was fun."

In case your sense of humor needs some science and facts to convince it to come out, here are what a couple of our favorite child development specialists have determined about play:

Dr. Daniel Hughes coined PACE (playful, accepting, curious, and empathetic) as a framework to help parents stay connected to children with challenging behaviors.[4] Playfulness helps develop trust and leaves the child in an open and engaged state of mind, receptive to their parents' guidance and love. When parents consistently maintain the attitude of PACE, they can relate to their child with greater patience and understanding. This leaves parents in a better position to respond to behavior, rather than react to it.

Dr. Karyn Purvis taught that playful engagement decreases the chemistry of fear and increases the chemistry of healing.[5]

It turns out humor reduces the distance between people and sparks trust. Your kids may find you more approachable when you're playful rather than stern and correcting.

> **Melissa**
> One time, after our daughter hit one of her siblings, I was able to pause before correcting her and think of a playful way to respond to the situation. She was expecting a lecture, but I calmly asked if I could see her hand. I then used a silly voice and started speaking to her hand like it was a person. "Hand, that wasn't very kind. You're supposed to be for helping, not for hurting." Then, I invited my daughter to join me in correcting her hand. Being a too-cool tween, my daughter just rolled her eyes, but my point was made while disarming her defenses with humor. I think the "hand" even apologized for hitting.
>
> We also use humor with our granddaughter. Whenever she's throwing a tantrum or crying, we'll scoop her up for a hug and then playfully pretend, in our most overdramatic way, to be upset that she's getting tears all over our clean clothes. She'll quickly flip to giggling and trying to wipe her face all over us. Once she's regulated, we can go back and address the issue at hand.

Laughter, which accompanies humor, also happens to be good for us. It increases blood flow, reduces muscle tension, and burns calories. In fact, in his TED Talk, Paul Osincup claims one minute of laughter burns as many calories as ten minutes on a rowing machine![6]

Practice Mindfulness

Mindfulness is a trending topic. If you type "mindfulness" into Google, it will return over 230 million hits. Some parents think of mindfulness as a calm-down tool but find it nearly impossible to implement in the moment. When you feel angry, it's difficult to focus on slow, intentional breathing. The solution is to make mindfulness part of your daily routine to support you when you're on the verge of becoming dysregulated.

Mindfulness for a Christian may be as simple as being very quiet before God and focusing on accepting your present situation exactly as it is. Psalm 46:10 (ESV) says,

> "Be still, and know I am God."

It's about resting in the sure knowledge that you are God's beloved child, and all is in His hands.

Regular mindfulness decreases activity in the parts of the brain responsible for impulsive reactivity, while increasing activity in the part of the brain responsible for more thoughtful and intentional responses.[7] We know you don't have many spare minutes, so be encouraged that even ten minutes of mindfulness can offer big results.[8]

One parent wrote to us, saying this:

> "Practicing meditation in the morning helps give me that second to pause, and focusing on my senses helps bring me back to the present and not flip my lid."

There are many different ways to practice mindfulness. We encourage you to do a little research and find something that works for you.

Decrease Your Mental Load

How often do you get interrupted during the day? Maybe you start to drink your coffee in the morning, only to find it sitting in the microwave at dinner time. Or do you start folding laundry but get sidetracked when a child needs a snack, or a sibling fight breaks out?

This amount of context switching affects your focus. More importantly, these decisions to switch tasks eat into your willpower. Eventually, decision fatigue sets in. This leads to decreased energy and focus, which may result in poor decision-making. When you hit decision fatigue, you're unlikely to parent with connection in mind. You may also lose your desire to be an empathetic parent.

Each decision you make throughout the day has a mental price. Unlike physical fatigue, which we often notice, decision fatigue happens unconsciously. Suddenly, you feel burnt out, and you stop caring.

While you can't control how often your kids interrupt you, simplifying other aspects of your life, such as food, your wardrobe, and your schedule, will reduce your overall mental load.

Food

The first area you can simplify is food, particularly dinner. Making dinner night after night can put a lot of stress on a parent. We find ourselves thinking, "What am I making for dinner?" all day if we don't have a plan in place.

Menu planning is a place to create simplicity. We encourage you to plan seven simple meals and assign each one a day of the week. Once you have that week's rotation down, and it becomes effortless, create a menu for a second week. Honestly, you can rotate those two weeks indefinitely, and most families will be just fine, as long as you make food they like. Or try having the same thing, preferably something you love, each day for breakfast or lunch. These simple plans reduce the number of decisions you need to make and ease just a little pressure in your days.

Another benefit to planning a menu is an increase in felt safety for your children. Posting the menu helps anxious kids or kids with trauma histories feel safer and more secure.

A final benefit of a meal rotation is simplified grocery shopping. And if you're not already ordering your groceries online, we strongly encourage you to give it a try.

Wardrobe

The second area you can simplify is your wardrobe. A quick way to simplify your wardrobe is to open your closet and take out everything you regularly wear: things that fit, are comfortable, are useful, and that you like. Set them aside. Then, put everything else in boxes or bags and put them away in the garage or storage area. As you live with the clothes you love, you'll begin noticing missing items. Go ahead and pull them out of the boxes. But overall, you're not likely to miss many of those things.

In a less stressful season of life, you can go through the stored items and decide what to keep or eliminate. For now, enjoy having fewer decisions to make each day when you get dressed.

Some parents find it helpful to create a "uniform." Kendra Adachi, author of *The Lazy Genius Way*, writes,

> "Deciding what to wear is comically hard, but doing it on a Monday morning is like being asked to cook Thanksgiving blindfolded. The solution? Have a Monday uniform. Choose one that makes you feel good whatever that means for you. . . . Mine is black jeans, a chambray shirt (no idea how to say chambray), and shoes that match the weather. Every. Single. Monday."[9]

Schedule

The third area to simplify is your family's schedule. We recommend creating an ideal week template that leads you through the week. For example, Monday is a stay-at-home day. When possible, don't schedule appointments or activities away from home. Use the day to reset your home and life from the weekend.

You may want to schedule a day for errands or a day for taking kids to the library or park. We find Fridays are a great day to meet with friends. Whatever structure you choose, use it to eliminate decisions and reduce stress. Once again, children who experienced early adversity will benefit from knowing the rhythm of the week and what the days will hold.

Lastly, create visual checklists for anything you do often, even things as simple as your morning and bedtime routines. While you can probably rattle off the steps involved, recalling them each morning and night is more mentally taxing than just following a written checklist.

> **Lisa**
> In addition to placing a framework around your week, you can also establish a daily structure by creating anchors.
>
> Anchors are solid, predictable events that hold the day in place. Anchors in the day provide kids with predictable structure, helping them feel calmer and more able to trust that their needs will be met and we will keep them safe. These anchors may not occur at exactly the same time each day (at least not for me), but they occur in the same order and same basic time period.
>
> When the children were young, and I homeschooled, those anchors were Breakfast, Quiet Hour, and Dinner. The children's routines flowed around these anchors. In the morning, they got up and dressed, did chores, helped with little ones, and then we paused.

Anchor #1: Breakfast

Following breakfast there was schoolwork, little ones playing, diapers, morning naps for babies, more chores, more playing, more schoolwork, morning snack, laundry, chores, schoolwork, lunch—you get the picture. Then, we paused again.

Anchor #2: Quiet Hour

Our Quiet Hour routine started with my two youngest being tucked in after a cup of milk, a story, and a few songs. Then, I read the Bible and books to elementary-age kids, followed by everyone heading to their own quiet spot with a stack of books. Older kids took their schoolwork or a good book and went to their rooms. This was my time to rest, read, or write.

One hour later, the house was busy again with schoolwork, playing, dinner prep, friends, chores, sports practices. When Russ walked in the door after work, we sat down at the table, pausing for the final anchor of the day.

Anchor #3: Dinner

As much as possible, we gathered as a family for dinner. We still had many young children home, and it was relatively easy to get most of the family around the table. There were routines with prayers, candles on the table, and everyone sharing about their day. We were also living within the realm of trauma with our little ones who had experienced early adversity, and dinner was difficult many nights. We simply did our best.

> Dinner flowed into bedtime and the day came to a close.
>
> These anchors gave our children solid places to pause each day. They knew a portion of the day had ended, and the next part was beginning. I also knew I had made it through a segment of the day, and whatever had happened, even if it was a disaster, it was done, and a new part of the day was beginning. I had a shot at starting over, and there were plenty of days when I needed it.
>
> Life looks a lot different now with my kids in school, but there are still anchors.
>
> *Anchor #1: School Prep and Breakfast*
>
> *Anchor #2: After School Snack/Homework*
>
> *Anchor #3: Dinner*

Our children still need the predictability of anchors in their days. Three-day weekends and school breaks are challenging for kids who are unsettled by changes in routine. They may be able to tolerate the lack of anchors on Saturday, and Sunday provides a few of its own, but add in a Friday or a Monday, and sometimes it's just too much.

Making a schedule and hanging it on the refrigerator, even for our middle schoolers, provides them with anchors and routines, relieving anxiety by letting them know what to expect.

Allow Yourself Unfocused Time

One result of high-stress parenting is that your brain may feel like mush. You probably have a to-do list a mile long but may find yourself wandering aimlessly around your house or resorting to scrolling through social media. Then, you feel guilty for not getting the laundry done or remembering to make something for dinner. As one parent says,

> "I'm relieved to know that I'm not 'crazy.' There's a reason I feel scattered and uncreative, have difficulty doing my job, and literally can't remember many things from the first year after we brought home our son. The brain is amazing."

For many busy parents, downtime seems like a waste of time. However, research shows we need unfocused time. Too much focus can repress our best thinking and productivity.[10] Have you ever had an "aha" moment in the shower or on the toilet? This is because you finally gave your brain a chance to work its magic.

When you're putting energy into focusing on something, your mind is working in a specific way. It's not making connections across the brain. But when your mind is wandering, it goes a little bit here, a little bit there, and starts mixing and matching things to create new ideas. To stay healthy and creative, you need time to let your mind wander or simply relax.

Just like decision fatigue, your brain also experiences focus fatigue. You start each morning with optimal capacity and deplete it throughout the day. However, if you alternate periods of focus and unfocus, you replenish your brain.

Unfocused time does not need to be still time. In fact, it's probably more effective if you're doing something low-key like gardening, walking, or folding laundry. To increase the effectiveness of your unfocused time, kick it off by creating a mental image of something positive.

According to another parent,

> "I have always known that cleaning the house, folding laundry, pulling weeds, and supervising the children as they ride bikes makes me feel better and less anxious, but I didn't realize that it has a lot to do with having some 'unfocused' time!"

When you are non-focused, without a specific goal, letting your mind wander or simply relax, you help the brain recharge, so it can handle the next challenging parenting situation with more ease.

Complete a Task

Dopamine is a neurotransmitter commonly known as the "happy hormone." Feeling like you're in a war zone with your kids each day can quickly zap the happy out of you.

As we mentioned earlier, dopamine is imperative for staying engaged as a parent. When you approach your kids for connection, and they consistently reject you, your brain becomes starved of dopamine. Your brain senses it might be dying, which kicks off a variety of anxiety-related responses, like blocked care.

One way to encourage your brain to release dopamine is to create a goal and accomplish it. This is why list-oriented people sometimes write down a task they've already done just so they can check it off. Recording a check mark gives your brain a hit of dopamine that can be addictive.

We'd encourage you to set three goals for the day to have the best chance of accomplishing them. The dopamine hit is greatest when you finish an entire list, no matter how small the list. It's better to finish a list of three than to have a list of eight and only get three finished.

You may find if you complete just one important task early in the morning, you'll feel satisfied with that success—even if the rest of the day falls apart.

Radically Accept Something about Your Situation

Radical acceptance is a practice that accepts something or someone just the way they are. It is not agreeing with or approving of a behavior, but it allows your brain to stop fighting against reality. It's also not giving up. The constant battle against your current reality is not only exhausting but also keeps your nervous system in a closed state, which means you are not doing your best problem solving or parenting.

Radical acceptance allows you to see areas where you can support or accommodate your kids, rather than fight to change them. It also has forced the word "should" out of our vocabulary. No more, "You're twelve! You should not be doing second-grade math for the third year in a row!" or "You should know by now you're staying forever."

We know it's counterintuitive, but radical acceptance can be the precursor to seeing a behavior or mindset change in your kids. Here are words from a couple of parents who are trying it:

> "I'm radically accepting that my daughter has brain trauma, and I need to let go of my expectations of what I thought my family would look like."

> "Today, I choose to accept that some days my kids can do age-appropriate things, and some days they can not. I will strive to meet them each day where they are and stop saying, 'You are X years old. You can do this.'"

Resurrect a Hobby or Start a New One

As we referenced earlier, when you allow yourself to be spontaneous or creative, playfully enjoying novel experiences, you begin creating new connections in your brain. Playfulness and fear cannot exist in your nervous system at the same time.

Reconnecting with an old hobby or starting a new one is much better for your brain than worrying about what could happen with your child in the future. You may be a much better parent when you take time to do something that sounds fun or uses a different part of your brain.

This chapter is packed with information and exercises because we believe a healthy mindset is a powerful key for overcoming blocked care. We encourage you to revisit the chapter as often as you need when you find compassion for yourself and your child fading.

Reflections and Practices for Chapter 6

Day 1: Find a Photo

This is one of our most powerful tools for overcoming blocked care. Your task is to find the earliest photo you have of your child. Or find a photo of your child that elicits compassion and positive emotions. Save it as wallpaper to your phone or print it out and put it somewhere where you'll see it.

> **Lisa**
> When I look at early photos of my children, I remember feeling I had so much love to give, and because I was such an experienced mom, I could heal the wounds in my kids' hearts. It hasn't been that simple, but when I see their sweet, and even sad, faces in early photos, my heart is moved with compassion.

> **Melissa**
> I had loads of compassion after initially reading each of our kids' profiles. I also remember seeing so much potential in our kids and feeling so confident they would be better off with us. Yes, we were pretty naive!

One mom wrote,

> "I put the first picture we took of our son on my phone's home screen and wallpaper. Each time I open my phone, the tears flow because I feel I've let him down in his healing journey. In a way, I'm relieved to feel the tears running down my face because it means I care about and love him. I'm not completely indifferent. The photo gives me hope."

As you look at the photo you chose, think back to the first time you heard your child's story or saw their face. What were you feeling?

This week, develop a habit of noticing the photo. Each time you see it, remember those early feelings of empathy and compassion.

Day 2: Look for Laughter

Do one thing that sounds fun or makes you laugh today. Make a note about what you did and how it made you feel in the space below.

Day 3: Practice Radical Acceptance

Choose one thing about your situation that you can radically accept. How will this change your thoughts, feelings, or response to situations? Journal about it in the space below.

Day 4: Decrease Your Mental Load

Choose one area of your life you could simplify and write down your first three steps. Is it feeding your family or just getting dressed each day?

Day 5: Read and Reflect

"As I'm tempted to wallow in guilt over all that I am not for my children, gently He points out that I was never meant to meet all their needs anyway. It isn't me who can make up for all their losses and hurts. He reminds me that I cannot be what they need Him to be: Savior. I quietly beg Him to fill in the gaps. Really, we are all crying out for the exact same thing: a true and consistent love that does not waver, a Savior who comes and binds up our wounds. Really, her heart is crying out for the exact thing I need myself, only her needs present on the surface, and mine are buried beneath a veil of performance, perfectionism, and pride. Hers come out messy and honest and desperate, and mine come out polished and deceiving and casual, as if I, too, am not craving a great rescue. I have so much to learn."[11]

Chapter 7: Immerse Yourself in Comfort and Beauty

This week, we're focusing on filling up your external world bucket. If your environment is adding stress to your life, you will have more difficulty staying engaged with the process of overcoming blocked care and connecting with your child.

Is there a place where you feel peaceful? Maybe it's a friend's home, a favorite vacation spot, or even a coffee shop. What is it about that place that allows you to experience more openness in your nervous system? Maybe you feel a lightness in your chest, the tension releasing in your shoulders, and your racing thoughts begin to slow. You may not be able to hop on a flight to your favorite escape, but you can make small changes to your environment that tell your nervous system it's safe to relax.

Let's go through your five basic senses and explore how they can cue safety to your nervous system.

Touch

Your tactile system is taking in data from sources, such as the clothes you wear, the temperature of your environment, and physical contact with pets or humans. Wear clothes that are comfortable and temperature appropriate. Melissa always says she's a grumpier parent in hard pants like jeans. Seek out a comforting human touch from safe people or pets. You might also find a weighted blanket or lap pad comforting and stress-reducing.

A warm hug at the end of a long day of parenting can give you strength to get up the next morning and do it all again. In the absence of someone to give you a hug, consider scheduling a massage. Some massage therapists even come to your home. Good touch is another way to cue safety to your nervous system, which helps you stay calm and regulated.

Sight

Be mindful of your visual field. When you look around your home, do you feel tension or peace? Are there particular areas of your home that feel good, while others make you want to run the other way? It can help to declutter at least a small corner in your home where your eyes are not distracted by too much visual stimulation.

Melissa's desk is in her bedroom, facing the bed, so she always makes the bed before starting work. Lisa can't focus on her day until the kitchen counters are clear. When there is too much stuff around our homes, and our spaces feel chaotic, we have less patience for the people we love.

Lighting is also important. Strings of soft white lights seem to induce happiness for many people. You could consider using smart light bulbs to dim lights and even change colors to match the energy needed for a particular time of day. If you find your spirits sinking as the sun goes down, put some lamps on timers that turn on before it's dark.

Another way to use your sense of sight to regulate your nervous system is to view the beauty of God's creation. Getting outside in nature has lots of benefits, but even viewing nature on a screen can help. One study shows viewing nature scenes improves your nervous system's ability to recover from a stressful interaction.[1] You may even try bringing nature inside with an easy-to-care-for succulent or other houseplant. Caring for a plant offers a surprising sense of purpose and joy, especially when the relationship with your child doesn't feel rewarding.

Hearing

What you are hearing plays a big part in how safe your nervous system feels. Think about how music is used in movies. There is a notable difference between music used to build suspense versus music during happy or joyful scenes. Playing music you love throughout the day can significantly increase your mood and reduce stress.

However, paying attention to what you listen to is about more than shifting your mood. Based on research by Dr. Stephen Porges, listening to specially filtered music is powerful enough to spontaneously shift your nervous system to a more open and socially available state.[2] We've helped hundreds of families use the Safe and Sound Protocol, a therapeutic listening program developed by Dr. Porges, to improve their relationships. Additionally, studies also show music can affect your heart rate, so playing music with 50 to 60 beats per minute may have a calming effect.[3]

Lastly, eliminate or dampen noises that could be overtaxing your nervous system and draining your energy. We're big fans of noise cancelling headphones and earplugs. If your house is often full of chaotic noise, be sure to incorporate periods of silence into your routine. While Melissa loves a good podcast when driving alone, she sometimes chooses to travel in silence. Lisa loves quiet and chooses taking a walk in silence when life is overwhelming. The lack of auditory input allows your brain to process both cognitively and emotionally, freeing up space for the hard work of rediscovering compassion for yourself and your child.

Smell

Smells are processed differently than the other four senses and have a stronger link to your emotions than any other sense. You can intentionally anchor a scent to an emotional experience. If there's a time of day when your relationship with your child is usually positive, add a scent ritual to your routine. You can add lavender lotion to a bedtime backrub or diffuse a specific essential oil whenever you enjoy a sweet treat with your child. Over time, your nervous system will associate that scent with affectionate feelings towards your child, so smelling that scent when you're having trouble staying compassionate may help you get back to being the parent you want to be.

We also love using pleasant scents as points of joy. Try smelling something minty or citrusy to energize you or uplift your mood. Peel an orange or crush some mint leaves between your fingers. Woody scents are calming and grounding. Take a walk in a pine forest or keep cedar blocks in your closet. Diffusing essential oils also provides a safe and easy way to inspire a certain mood in your home.

Taste

We don't always think about tastes in our environment, but we didn't want to leave out the fifth sense. Different from nutrition, this is more about the sensory experience of what's in our mouth. Think about what tastes or textures spark joy. You might prefer crunchy and salty while someone else lives for sweet and creamy. Some people like cinnamon gum while others prefer the minty varieties. We both feel energized by a cold, sparkling water in the afternoon. Find tastes that appeal to you.

Do your best to create an environment that meets the needs of all your senses. This will fill the bucket for your external world, making it easier to keep working on the relationship with your child.

Reflections and Practices for Chapter 7

Day 1: Get Comfy

How does your touch (tactile) system cue your nervous system that you are safe? Ask yourself what feels good to you today. Do you need to take off those jeans that are a bit too tight and put on comfy pants? Would resting under a weighted blanket for ten minutes feel calming?

What helps you feel safe and calm? Is it a weighted blanket, warm socks, or loose clothes? Is it a tight hug or a light hand on your shoulder? Spend a little time exploring this.

Day 2: Declutter One Space

Improve your visual field by decluttering something from your house. It can be large, like the piece of furniture that's never fit in your home and makes the room seem crowded. Take a picture of it and list it on an online sale site. Or call your local thrift shop and schedule to have it picked up.

Maybe it's something smaller, like the overflowing box of mismatched socks in your laundry room. Take five to ten minutes to match socks, and throw the rest away. We give you permission to let them go.

How about the stack of papers on your kitchen counter or desk? Sort it into three piles: trash, file, not sure if you need. With the papers you're not sure about, take a picture (or create a pdf with your phone), and then throw them away.

If you need a quick and simple decluttering task, grab a plastic grocery bag and spend five minutes quickly moving through your house picking up anything that can be thrown away and tossing it in the bag. When your timer rings, tie the bag, and throw it in the trash.

And if you've been driving around for weeks with a bag of items for the thrift store in the back of your car, this is the perfect day to drop it off!

What did you declutter? How do you feel as a result? Journal about it in the space below.

Day 3: Listen for Safety

What types of sounds cue safety to your nervous system? Sometimes, people need calming instrumental music or nature sounds. Other times, they may need upbeat music to sing along to or even loud rhythmic music that matches the intensity of their feelings. Lisa loves listening to playlists created for different times of the day.

Find what works for you and intentionally surround yourself with helpful sounds today.

Day 4: Smell Something Good

Find something to smell that brings up happy feelings. Diffuse a favorite essential oil, or light a candle you love. Spritz on the perfume, or use the special lotion you've been saving for special occasions. Buy yourself flowers. If you're feeling ambitious, bake or cook something that fills your home with a scent that also fills your heart.

Day 5: Read and Reflect

"Entering into creation is how we attune our ears to the creative nudges, how we notice the stirrings of inspiration . . . Not only can we allow ourselves to be awestruck by the beauty of a bird song, a crocus bud, or a tulip, but we can also take in the vastness, allow ourselves to breathe in the openness, and make space for our souls to expand."[4]

Chapter 8:
Lean into God

Building a connected relationship with your child takes an incredible amount of energy. Practicing radical compassion is taxing to your brain because it requires you to be curious and insightful. You may also be restructuring your life and creating new routines to reduce stress in your home.

This level of therapeutic parenting takes a toll on your body. You may find yourself needing to eat differently, find time for movement each day, or try to get more sleep.

Friendships, especially with people who truly understand your parenting journey, are invaluable. An online community of like-minded parents can be a lifesaver. But at the end of the day, there isn't a person in the world who can provide all you need to keep going, keep loving, and keep pursuing connection.

Your connection to God offers you strength for the seemingly impossible task of parenting a child with early adversity. You are loved and precious to your Father. He sees how hard you're working to be the parent your child needs.

> **Lisa**
>
> I remember a conversation I had with an adoptive mom of two young children from foster care. With grown kids and now in her early fifties, she and her husband didn't go into foster care hoping to adopt, but they loved these kids. When it became clear the children could not return to their original family, these empty nesters said, "Yes," to being a forever family.
>
> And you know what? It's beautiful. And it's really hard. This mom told me people have questioned whether they made the right decision. Did they really hear God? After all, this appears to be a bit of a disaster.
>
> I replied that the folks asking those questions need to read the Bible. Time and again in scripture, we read of people who follow God with all their hearts and yet suffer. Hardship is their companion. There are so many examples, but today, the apostle Paul comes to mind. He was beaten, stoned, shipwrecked, imprisoned, sleepless, hungry, and thirsty. Following Jesus did not make his life easy. It cost him everything.
>
> There is a cost to being used by God. You cannot enter a child's suffering without suffering in some way too. Trauma is messy and spills over onto the ones willing to come near. Yet you have immersed yourself in it in the name of love.

Foster and adoptive parents, you are being used by God. You are a shelter for children needing to know they are precious, valued, and loved. When they look in your eyes and see warmth and acceptance, they begin to trust you, which is foundational for healing.

I know many of you face hardships as a result of saying, "Yes," to caring for vulnerable children. Don't lose heart; hold on. As the apostle Paul wrote, "your labor is not in vain" (1 Cor. 15:58, ESV).

Melissa

I grew up in a Christian family. When things got challenging after we adopted, I wanted to believe God was in control. I remember praying and fasting. But if I'm being completely honest, I was putting most of my trust and faith into finding the "right" trauma-informed resource. I was convinced if my kids did neurofeedback or Eye Movement Desensitization and Reprocessing (EMDR), it would "fix" the situation.

When we were visiting with the family who would eventually provide long-term respite for one of our daughters, I asked the mom what training she had and if she knew of Dr. Karyn Purvis. It's embarrassing now, but I remember inwardly scoffing when she told me she prayed herself and the kids through the tough times. In hindsight, I wish I had been more rooted in my own spiritual care during this time.

As people of faith, our foundation is our relationship with God. He is our secure base and safe haven. We want to share simple practices for staying connected to God. We are fully aware that your brain is stressed and learning new things is nearly impossible, so let's focus on small steps to stay connected to God in a time when you need him most.

Worship

In some contexts, worship becomes synonymous with singing. Psalm 29:1–2 (NIV) says,

> "Ascribe to the Lord, you heavenly beings, ascribe to the Lord glory and strength. Ascribe to the Lord the glory due his name; worship the Lord in the splendor of his holiness."

There are many other forms of worship as well:

- creating or enjoying art
- feasting and celebrating
- serving others
- journaling/writing
- praying

In a recent workshop on blocked care, a dad shared that he spends time in nature watching for what he calls "glimpses of glory."

However you choose to worship, we encourage you to find a way that brings joy and feels nearly effortless to you.

Prayer

Adoption and foster care may lead you to places you never imagined. It's no ordinary life, friends. We often find ourselves telling God, "I just don't know what to do." In his wonderful book, *A Praying Life*, Paul Miller writes "A needy heart is a praying heart."[1] Prayer is for helpless people. Prayer is for the weary. Prayer is for hearts once filled with compassion but now closed and maybe even hard.

Your life is filled with tasks, appointments, and needs—so many needs. How do you make time for prayer? Paul Miller also writes, "Learning to pray does not offer us a less busy life, it offers us a less busy heart."[2]

If you're anything like us, it's easy to find time to worry and talk to friends about parenting challenges. You may also spend hours researching problems you're facing with your kids. You may not be too busy to pray, but prayer requires you to get quiet, and this is the challenge.

WHY PRAY?

1. You Need Wisdom

The Word says,

> "If any of you lacks wisdom, let him ask God, who gives generously to all without reproach, and it will be given him" (James 1:5 ESV).

We need wisdom, and we're guessing you do too. Sometimes, you may be desperate to hear from God because there are so many options you don't know what to choose. Other times, you have run out of options, and there is nowhere to turn. But God says He generously gives wisdom when you ask.

2. You Need Hope

Remember that God is in this with you, and He has a good plan. Your life is not random, and your child didn't just happen to end up in your family. Even when you doubt yourself, God has confidence in you. He chose you to be your child's parent. You were made for this job.

3. You Need an Awareness of God—You Are Not Alone

In the middle of the night when the world is sleeping, and you're lying awake with the weight of worry on your chest, remember that you aren't alone. When kindness toward your child has all but dried up, you need Jesus. Prayer leads you to the arms of your Father and will remind you of His constant presence.

4. You Can Be Honest

Good news! You don't need to act holy or clean yourself up before you pray. Prayer is a "come as you are" affair. God knows you, really knows you, so you might as well pour it all out, every thought, fear, and doubt. Nothing surprises God, not one tiny thing. And He loves you no matter what.

5. You'll Find Rest

Jesus tells us in Matthew 11:28 (ESV),

> "Come to me all you who are weary and heavy laden, and I will give you rest."

When you take your worries and heaviness and lay them down before the Lord, your heart and mind can rest. Of course, this laying down process is continual – each day and sometimes each minute. We often find ourselves praying, "I give this to you," each time the worry comes back to our minds.

WHAT IF YOU FEEL YOU CAN'T PRAY?

Over the years we've found three simple ways to pray when life is too hard and we're discouraged, or we're too busy and overwhelmed. In the darkest days of our lives, these simple ways of praying held us close to God when we could hardly get through the days.

3 WAYS TO PRAY

1. Pray without Ceasing

It may seem counterintuitive, but when you're completely overwhelmed, you need to pray without ceasing. You may be thinking, "What? How is it even possible?" The apostle Paul wrote in his letter to the Thessalonians:

"'Rejoice always, pray without ceasing, give thanks in all circumstances; for this is the will of God in Christ Jesus for you' (1 Thess. 5:16–18 ESV)."

One way to pray without ceasing is through a practice called breath prayer. Pray a simple phrase, short enough to be said in one breath, repeating it over and over as needed. It's that simple. Here are a few examples:

"Lord, have mercy."

"'My help comes from the maker of heaven and earth' (Ps. 121:2 NIV)."

"'When I am afraid, I will trust in you' (Ps. 56:3 NKJV)."

"'Not my will, but yours' (Luke 22:42 NIV)."

"Lord, Jesus Christ, Son of God, have mercy on me."

2. Hold Them Before the Lord

Simply hold the person before the Lord in your mind. Imagine them at the foot of the cross or in the arms of Jesus. When you don't know what to pray or don't have the right words, the Holy Spirit does. Take your thoughts, words, and hopes to the throne of your good Father. Romans 8:26–27 (NIV) says,

"In the same way, the Spirit helps us in our weakness. We do not know what we ought to pray for,

> but the Spirit himself intercedes for us through wordless groans. And he who searches our hearts knows the mind of the Spirit, because the Spirit intercedes for God's people in accordance with the will of God."

3. Pray a Psalm

When you're at a loss for words, pray a psalm by simply reading it, silently or aloud, and claiming the words for yourself. Consider Psalm 23; words like this may comfort you:

> "'Even though I walk through the valley of the shadow of death, I will fear no evil, for you are with me; your rod and your staff, they comfort me' (Ps. 23:4 ESV)."

Psalm 13 is also beautiful, ending with these two verses:

> "'But I have trusted in your steadfast love; my heart shall rejoice in your salvation. I will sing to the LORD because he has dealt bountifully with me' (Ps. 13: 5–6 ESV)."

With 150 Psalms to choose from, you're sure to find one that expresses your heart and thoughts.

In the hardest and most overwhelming times, don't give up on prayer. Try these three simple ways of praying. Draw close to the Father, and He will always meet you.

The Word

The Bible is central to our relationship with God. There are many reasons to read God's Word, including:

- learning of God's character and how He loves us
- finding wisdom
- being reminded of foundational truths
- finding hope
- being reminded of how we should live
- becoming fruitful
- gaining courage

There are also lots of methods you could consider to help you establish and maintain the habit of reading the Bible. You could:

- choose a translation easy for your brain or new to you.
- follow a daily reading plan.
- use a devotional, such as *Faith, Hope, & Connection*, edited by us and written by thirty different adoptive parents.
- use an app to read God's Word easily wherever you are.
- listen to sermons.
- keep your Bible open on the kitchen counter and read a short portion several times throughout the day to nourish your soul.
- post meaningful verses on index cards or sticky notes above your kitchen sink or on your mirror.
- listen to scripture set to music.

As we serve adoptive families, we are keenly aware of how much we need to rely on Jesus. When parents have exhausted all the tools or practical tips they know, and life is still hard, Jesus remains.

Reflections and Practices for Chapter 8

Day 1: Ask God for Help

How would you like God to help you in this healing journey? Tell Him.

Day 2: Worship in New Ways

How do you best connect with God in worship? Are there new ways you want to try? Spend 10 minutes worshiping God in the way you feel led.

Day 3: Consider Breath Prayer

What word, phrase, or scripture could you use as a simple breath prayer? Write it below and memorize it. Let it become a simple prayer.

Day 4: Become Aware of God's Presence

In the last day or two, when or where were you most aware of God's presence?

Day 5: Read and Reflect

"Waiting on God in the silent places of the soul is an active waiting that contains a seed of expectancy and hope. We wait with the kind of anticipation a night watchman feels as he waits for the morning sun to signal the end of his watch. No matter how many hours of darkness he has to wait through, the watchman knows from experience that morning will come."[3]

Chapter 9: Surround Yourself with Life-Giving People

When your relationship with your kids is tricky, it's important to have other safe relationships supporting you. You need someone to care for you, someone who can calm your defensive nervous system and help you regulate your emotions. This person can be a professional therapist or another seasoned parent who has walked through a similar experience and come out the other side.

> **Lisa**
> The struggles we were facing with our children seemed insurmountable. I began to question everything I had thought to be true of myself as a mother. The image I had carried of being a good mom began to fall. A professional suggested parenting classes, a pastor asked me if I was giving up on one of our children, and our homeschooling friends thought we had lowered the bar far too much.

> I'll never forget the first time we met with a therapist who really understood adoption. I talked for a long time about the challenges we were facing and how desperate we were for help. When I finally paused, she leaned forward, looked at me with compassion, and said, "But how are you doing in all of this?" I burst into tears. Her compassion immediately made me feel safe, which allowed me to trust her. We went on to work with her for years.

In the book, *What Happened to You*, by Oprah Winfrey and Dr. Bruce Perry, they write, "Our major finding is that your history of relational health—your connectedness to family, community, and culture—is more predictive of your mental health than your history of adversity . . . Connectedness has the power to counterbalance adversity."[1]

We know you don't have much margin to add more relationships to your life, but finding safe and life-giving people is imperative to maintaining resilience in your nervous system. Fellow adoptive parents who are a little ahead of you in the journey can be a wonderful source of support. Extended family and friends who have known you for a long time are a treasure. They can be part of your circle of support.

Remember that God designed us to be in relationship.

Two parents reached out to us and commented,

> "I scheduled a trip to visit my sister. I realized that I was shut off from friends and have cut all ties. How did that happen?"

> "I met with a friend the other night. I was feeling isolated from friends and to be honest, I felt judged by anyone I disclosed to about how things were really going, so I have been disconnected. But it was wonderful. I could have cried when she asked me how I was really doing."

Do you feel isolated? These are some of our favorite ways to stay connected to life-giving people:

Early morning walks with your spouse or a friend

We love this option because it efficiently kills two birds with one stone. You get to move your body *and* stay connected. Try to set a schedule, so you can take the planning off your mental plate.

Lunch or coffee dates while the kids are in school

The benefit of connecting with friends or your spouse during school hours is that you don't have to worry about childcare. Lisa meets with three of her closest friends for coffee on the first Wednesday morning of each month. It may not seem like much, but the consistency keeps them connected.

In-person support groups

Shame can get out of control in isolation. Support groups are a great place to find other parents with similar situations and experiences. Some counties run local foster parent groups. Check with your local church for other support groups.

Virtual support groups

While we recommend trying to see people in real life, virtual groups can be life-giving too. We love video apps because they allow you to connect and co-regulate with people's faces and voices. Video messaging apps are perfect for busy parents because each person can listen and respond as they have time, in a way that fits their schedule.

Therapist and/or spiritual director

Enneagram expert Suzanne Stabile is known for saying everyone should have a therapist and a spiritual director. We agree! Therapists are trained to help you navigate your relationships with other people. Even if you don't have a specific issue to work through, a regular appointment with a therapist or counselor is a great place to verbally process or just rant without spending too much relationship capital with your friends or spouse.

A spiritual director is a supportive companion to you as you explore and nurture your relationship with God. They will lead you in the work of spiritual formation which is the process of opening your heart more fully to God. Michael John Cusick writes, "The work of spiritual formation is to tend the gap between what we believe and what we experience."[2] There may be no more important time for this than when healing from blocked care.

As you surround yourself with lifegiving people, we hope you'll remember how good it feels to have relationships that bring you joy. Spending time with friends and family who fill you—and don't deplete you—will create more margin in your nervous system to continue the process of overcoming blocked care.

Reflections and Practices for Chapter 9

Day 1: Identify Your Life-giving People

List the people you and your child come into regular contact with, whether they're helpful or not. Think about household members, friends and extended family, professionals, and community members (this could be doctors, therapists, teachers, your faith community, etc.), and people or groups where you find support virtually.

Next, list at least one positive impact they're having on you or your child's life. Maybe you feel like your spouse never helps or contributes. But do they provide a paycheck each month? Maybe you feel like your friends are constantly judging you, but do they provide a place where your child behaves or feels accepted and successful?

This is what other parents have told us about this exercise:

> "The biggest takeaway from today's exercise was realizing how much support we actually do have."
>
> "I'm really blessed to see how many people I do have as support, and to focus on the 'professional' section a bit, as there are not too many in there. Such a helpful activity!!!"
>
> "I have great support even though most of my village isn't informed too much about trauma. I need to focus on what I have—not on what I don't."
>
> "I am definitely guilty of thinking we don't really have a tribe who 'gets it,' but listing the people in our regular interactions helped

me see we have more support than I realized. I need to be better about asking for help/support when it's needed."

"I think something I learned from writing down these people is they almost all have (spiritual, temperamental) gifts I do not possess. And most of the younger kids in the family are very calm and regulating presences. Alternately, they have a kind of energy to match our own kiddo's—neither of which I feel I often have."

"This practice helped me see all of the support we do have. Living overseas in a country where adoption and special needs aren't widely recognized and there is, in general, no community support for local people, it's so important for me to remember the ways God has provided very specifically for our needs for support here."

"What a great exercise to do. I see on paper how much support I really have."

"Thinking this through, I realized every person in my life plays a different role. Some are available to give me respite; some are encouragers; some have walked in my shoes before and understand, so they have empathy and advice from their own experience; some are in my son's life and have shown care even though they see his struggles; some are good listeners; some are really my cheerleaders."

"This helped me to realize my tribe is bigger than I realized. I think because our tribe does not look a certain way (the way I would like it to look), I too easily dismiss the support we do have."

"My biggest take away from this exercise was feeling the desire to reconnect with friends and family that I haven't reached out to in a while. There aren't many people I'm in regular contact with, so I made a list of people who are special to me. I reached out to three people I wouldn't have contacted if it weren't for this exercise. The most meaningful was my uncle who I haven't talked to in years. He was thrilled to hear from me. It sparked wonderful memories from my childhood. I needed the connection and reminder today. He even sent me a picture of myself drawing with him, a favorite hobby of mine when I was younger. It was nice to be reminded of happy memories."

"I'm still thinking about the different roles individuals can play in my children's life. I've been so caught up in thinking about consistency, about developing routines, and setting up structures for expected behavior, that I have been pushing away sources of support which might provide something different—even if it means they'll 'get away with' the behavior we are trying to contain. Feels important to figure out how to balance the place for these outlets."

Use the space below to make your list.

Day 2: Reach Out to a Friend You Haven't Talked to in a While

It can be a simple text or call. Take a moment to connect with someone who knows you. A friend who can make you laugh, or one who will pray for you is just what you need.

Who will you call or text?

Day 3: Plan a Date with a Friend

Put it on the calendar even if it's going to be a month before it happens. You'll have something to look forward to as the day approaches. Make arrangements for your kids in advance, so you aren't panicking as the day gets closer. It's worth the effort.

Day 4: Schedule an Appointment with a Therapist or Spiritual Director

Many therapists and spiritual directors meet with people online. It's wonderful to meet with someone in person, but if there are too many roadblocks to make that happen, don't hesitate to schedule an online appointment.

Day 5: Read and Reflect

"Connection with others is about a sense of belonging and creating a shared sense of safety. Belonging is not just a psychological state, it's a biological need. Social connection is a necessary ingredient for a life of well-being."[3]

Chapter 10: Connect with Your Child

Now that you've started filling up your other buckets, we want to give you ideas to create new, more positive relationship patterns with your kids, starting with your foundation of fun.

Create a Foundation of Fun

A family's foundation of fun is created with daily or weekly rituals everyone enjoys, and they should happen no matter what. When we say, "no matter what," we mean that these fun things or activities are not removed for bad behavior. They are things you do because you value positivity, connection, relationship, and/or fun in your family.

Many of our kids have learned to be transactional rather than relational. Even positive reinforcement further cements this paradigm of transactionalism. I do something bad, something bad happens. I do something good, something good happens. Foundation of fun helps to reverse this. This is good stuff happening even after or despite bad behavior. Plus, it's healthy to have fun.

Another side benefit of creating this foundation of fun is increased maturity in our kids. Dr. Bruce Perry says maturity is built through positive social-emotional interactions.[1] Dr. Mona Delahook, a licensed clinical psychologist, concurs. "By providing positive, enriching experiences for children we help them build their house of social and emotional development, one step at a time."[2]

If your child has a fragile nervous system or you have children spanning a wide age gap, you may have to build a foundation of fun with each child or in smaller groups. If your child struggles often, try creating a foundation of fun that happens frequently.

> **Melissa**
> During a season when one of our sons was really struggling, I started an hourly ritual of giving him an aromatherapy hand massage, followed by one mindfulness activity from an iPad app. A timer would go off at the top of every hour, and we'd stop whatever we were doing to pause for some oils and mindfulness.
>
> I don't know about your kids, but ours rarely want to use the tools available to them once they are fully dysregulated. They never want to stop for deep breathing or a walk outside. They just want to stay mad! The beauty of having a foundation of fun is that it becomes a part of the routine but may pop up at the perfect time to pattern interrupt a dysregulated moment. One day, our

son was stomping angrily around the house when the timer indicated it was time to take a break.

"The timer dinged!" I called cheerily, "Do you want to start with mindfulness or a hand massage?"

"The iPad," he begrudgingly chose.

Five minutes later, after he completed a mindfulness game, I asked, "How are you feeling now?"

"I actually feel a lot better," he admitted.

"Mmm . . . " I mused out loud, "It seems like the game helped you calm down when you were angry."

Here are some other creative and fun ideas from our community:

"This felt tricky at first because of our big age gap—teens and an immature 6-year-old make for a difficult space to all have regular fun together. . . . but, daily we are thinking funny videos, and weekly doing a themed activity such as: movie night with a themed dinner (first will be the new Lady and Tramp with spaghetti and meatballs, etc.), night of cupcake wars, campfire and s'mores, family Olympic games, etc."

"Daily: Fart jokes, funny videos, 1 prank. Weekly: Taco Tuesday, Weiner Wednesday, Pizza Friday, gardening, movie night."

"We created a family handshake we do before school each morning."

> **Lisa**
> My friend, Andrea, greets her children with glass bottles of special root beer and cookies each Friday after school. No matter how well or poorly the week has gone, whether behavior has been good or not so great, her kids know that as the school week ends, they will come together as a family and enjoy a special treat. She says, "It's no matter what. They can count on this consistent love waiting for them."

Regulate Together

Providing our children with experiences that are responsive, rhythmic, and repetitive can help them build a stronger capacity to regulate and tolerate frustration.[3]

Another way to think about this is Repetition + Rhythm + Relationship = Regulation.

Repetitive means the activity has inherent repetition *and* it happens repetitively over time in your child's routine. For example, walking happens through repetitive steps and could happen every weekday.

Rhythmic means it has a predictable rhythm, like melodic music instead of improv. Pool time is rhythmic if you're doing bobs or swimming laps, as opposed to free play.

Relational means the activity happens within a safe, responsive relationship. You may send your children outside to jump on the trampoline. Jumping is rhythmic and repetitive. If you join them in jumping, it also becomes relational.

Any combination of these Rs is good, but all three together are the most powerful!

> **Lisa**
> My favorite tool for regulation is a rocking chair. I've rocked babies and toddlers and even my bigger kids. Rocking recreates the movement our children experienced in utero. Rocking is rhythmic, repetitive, and relational. You can rock while singing, reading a book, eating a snack, or soothing a dysregulated child. It's as calming for you as it is for them.

Other parents in our community shared ideas like these:

"A couple of my boys beg to play catch with me, and I think I know why it's so enjoyable to them now!! I will definitely make it more of a priority."

"Our nine- year-old has always liked to have his back rubbed. He struggles to shut down his brain at night, and this seems to help."

"My seventeen-year-old daughter is not very keen on being active. However, she does enjoy dancing, so I will make sure we do dance parties more often! My twenty-one-year-old started asking if we can throw a netball ball together. I now understand the impact this repetitive action can have. I'll try to do it daily."

"We ride bikes or swim daily with my eleven-year-old. He also loves drumming. We play music together and take turns creating a beat for the rest of us to try. We also play squash and tennis. We swing, jump on a trampoline, dance, do yoga, hike, pet and groom our dog and cats."

"We just gave the kids basketballs for Christmas, so I am going to see if he will dribble and play bounce pass with me when I can see him starting to struggle."

"We have 'jam sessions' (I would play guitar and/or sing along)."

If you don't have a lot of space or need to have your child sit still through church or school, keep lots of gum on hand. The chewing is rhythmic and repetitive, and you can get in on the fun, too!

"You're fun to be around"

When your kids aren't fun to be around, you may become a parent who is not fun to be around either. Watch for a moment when you can genuinely tell your child, "You're fun to be around." This can break the negative interaction cycle and promote positive interactions.

Your children have wounded hearts, and it can take a lot of effort to fill them with encouragement. Some of your kids may also be adept at turning a compliment around into something negative.

> **Lisa**
> We were working hard to encourage our daughter and continue building upon some progress we'd made in our relationship. Our therapist suggested three things I could say or do, and I wrote them down in my notebook, waiting for a chance to try them.
>
> That week, her glasses broke, so amid the back-to-school flurry, we raced to the eye doctor to pick out new frames.

We had a lovely pocket of time open to the two of us, and I wanted to capitalize on it. She loved food of all kinds, and I hadn't eaten lunch, so we walked across the parking lot to Subway to share a sandwich. I let her choose what we ate, although I left the jalapenos off my half; my girl could handle some incredibly spicy food.

I wanted to remember exactly what the therapist said, and thankfully I had my notebook in my purse, so I ran to the bathroom to review my notes. I know it's sort of silly, but I didn't want to miss this opportunity by forgetting my goals. Number one on my list was to tell her how fun she is to be around. I couldn't say it if it wasn't true, but in that moment, she was truly fun to be with.

As a side note, the therapist reminded us that when she was not fun to be around, we became parents who weren't fun to be around either. How very true. I was not the mother I wanted to be when I was in survival mode.

I went back to the table, where she had laid out our sandwiches and gotten us each a cup of water. We talked about lots of things, and then I said, "You know what? It's so fun being here with you. I've really noticed how fun it is to be around you at home too. You're bringing so much happiness to us."

If you could have seen her face, you would have gotten tears in your eyes like I got in mine. She beamed and even looked a little shy. It was so simple to meet this deep need of her heart—to know she is loved and enjoyed by me.

> Don't we all need this? We want our spouses and friends to want to spend time with us. We don't want to be a task on someone's to-do list. We want our adult kids to keep coming around, not because they must but because they enjoy being with us.
>
> Watch for a moment when you can tell your child, "You're fun to be around," or "I'm having fun with you." Just saying it will be good for your heart, and maybe you'll get a sweet response like I got.

Give a Small Gift

Generosity is challenging when we feel depleted from caring for our children. But the act of generosity is good for us even when it doesn't make sense. If you've been parenting with your heart closed, and all compassion has evaporated, perhaps being generous and giving a small gift will be good for your heart.

One parent told us,

> "After a terrible morning before school, I was at the store and saw there was a ball on clearance for fifty cents—perfect. I gave it to him after school—he was pleased. This was the last thing I wanted to do after the morning—but grace."

Giving a small gift can make your kids feel cared for. If you add the words, "I saw this in the store, and it made me think of you," it adds to the power of the gift. It lets them know you have them on your mind when you're not with them.

Melissa

One of our daughters feels the most loved through gifts. If you have a big family or are on a tight budget, gift giving may feel impractical or overwhelming. When she lived at home, she routinely ate a banana every morning with breakfast. I started buying a bunch of bananas each week specifically for her. I'd present them with a little flourish and smile and watch her face light up at receiving something bought especially for her. The best part was that it didn't cost me anything extra out of our budget to delight her each week.

Lisa

My kids went back to school this week. Last time I went grocery shopping, I picked up a large pack of gum for each of them—the kind in a hard plastic case with tons of pieces. I tied a ribbon around the gum with a note saying, "Have a great first day!" This was less than $2.00 per kid, but I know it is appreciated and used—even if I don't get a response like, "Hey Mom, you're so great. Thanks so much for buying me my favorite gum!"

Give with an open hand and heart because you don't know how your child will respond. Will her face light up, even for a moment, when she receives your gift? Will he open it and throw it on the floor saying, "This is stupid!"? You can't control their response; you can only control our own.

Give an Unexpected "Yes"

Giving your children an unexpected "yes" is powerful for interrupting negative interactions and increasing connection. So often, they ask for something, and the default answer is "No." Surprise them with a "Yes!"

> **Lisa**
> One busy August day, I paused in the middle of a project to pick my son up from the pool. As he got in the car, he asked, "Will you take me to get cleats? Football practice begins next week."
>
> My immediate thought was, "I don't have time for that right now!" But before I said a word, I remembered the power of an unexpected yes. I said, "I have time to go to one store. Do you want to look and see if we find what you need?"
>
> He looked so surprised and happy. We walked into the store and found one pair of Nike cleats in his size. He loved them, and I was thrilled to find they were on clearance for $14.95.
>
> This was a great moment of connection for us and a good reminder that giving an unexpected yes might have even more benefits than we imagine.

Here are some stories other parents shared with us after giving an unexpected "Yes":

> "Yes to a movie and to Laffy Taffys. You would have thought I'd given her $1,000:)"

> "We're pretty strict on no food in bedrooms because of the inevitable mess, but when my son came up to me and said, 'Mom, we're making a party in my room. Can we eat breakfast in there?' and I heard my other son muttering under his breath, 'I know they'll say no.' I said 'Yes, where do you want your plate?' He was so excited. Afterwards, they wrote us a note that said, 'I love you mom and dad' and cut it out in the shape of a heart. My husband and I got to eat a quiet breakfast together, and it was really sweet listening to the boys giggling away in the other room."

> "I was already treating my son to a late lunch out when he asked for a dessert treat too. Normally, I would have said no, but I just ordered it to go. The look on his face—priceless! Win."

> "So seriously, I'm all about reading . . . but I have such a hard time with all the 'dumb' books the school has at the book fair! I took a deep breath and said YES to a Super Mario Brothers book and a Pokémon book for my two boys!! At least they're reading!"

Stories like this from parents always delight us.

Comforting Touch

Known as the "love" or "cuddle" hormone, oxytocin plays a key role in both attachment and empathy. Oxytocin can be released through soothing physical contact, music, or movement.[4] Because oxytocin can be released in multiple ways, you can stimulate your child's oxytocin system through touch, even if you're experiencing blocked care.

Whether you need a calming tool to incorporate into your everyday routine or a quick, effective, back-pocket intervention during a period of dysregulation, a hand massage technique is an invaluable tool for adoptive and foster families. We recommend sticking with one that is repetitive and predictable. Maybe start with thumb circles on the palm and back of the hand, followed by gently squeezing each finger from the knuckle to the tip. Try adding an essential oil for additional benefits.

Here are some reasons why we're such fans of hand massages:

1. They are less triggering than affectionate touch.

We already talked about how warm touch stimulates the release of the hormone oxytocin, which enhances a sense of trust and attachment and can be a crucial component of healing. However, for kids with attachment challenges, physical affection like hugs can be triggering rather than healing. Hand massages are just clinical enough, while still delivering all the benefits of touch. For especially fragile kids, you may need to avoid eye contact while giving the massage.

2. They are rhythmic and repetitive.

The realm of the unknown, even not knowing what will be served for dinner, can be dysregulating for kids who have a history of early adversity. Once your child has experienced a hand massage, they can rely on the predictability and feel confident because they know exactly what to expect the next time around.

3. They can be done almost anywhere.

Hands are easy to access in public places, making a quick hand massage the perfect way to connect quickly on the go.

4. They benefit both the caregiver and child.

Research by Tiffany Field, director of the Touch Research Institute, demonstrates that the person giving a massage experiences as great a reduction in stress hormones as the person on the receiving end.[5]

Because connection needs to happen before correction, try creating a habit of utilizing this hand massage technique as a buffer before correcting a behavior.

Child-Directed Time

One result of trauma is feeling out of control. Your kids might fight for control as a self-protective mechanism to feel safer. If your own nervous system is activated, your natural response is to push back against any efforts your kids make to take control. A nasty control battle often ensues. We encourage you to carve out time when you let your kids run the show—at least for a couple minutes.

One parent told us,

> "This made a huge difference in our foster daughter's behavior, language development, and attachment. Playing with her and

> following her lead made me feel like I was doing something to be a good mom."

It may feel counterintuitive, but sharing an appropriate amount of control with our kids is healthy. One way we can do it is by being intentional about child-directed time. This is a set amount of time when you follow your child's lead, as long as it's safe. Our mirroring of their activity is a powerful way to strengthen attachment.

For younger kids, narrate what they're doing, but refrain from asking questions. For example, you might say, "There goes the blue car!" But don't say, "Can you find the blue car?"

For older kids, ask to join them in something they're doing or that you know they'll like. It might be learning to play the newest video game or listening to their music on a car ride. Try to resist the urge for commentary on their choices. One mom told us about getting a tattoo with her older adopted child. You may not take a child-led experience this far, but the concept remains the same.

Do an Act of Kindness

Practicing kindness toward your children may feel difficult when you are completely burned out. But if you can push yourself to start, you may find it comes more naturally over time.

Kindness has so many benefits for your nervous system and your relationships.

1. Acts of kindness release dopamine and serotonin in your brain, which help keep your caregiving systems activated.[6]

2. Kindness enhances the release of oxytocin between two people which is a powerful bonding hormone.[7]

3. Kindness promotes compassion, the very thing you need right now. Compassion helps build connection, which is exactly what you want with your children.

4. Kindness increases your sense of belonging.

Dr. Ritchie Davidson, a professor of psychology and psychiatry from the University of Wisconsin, says, "It's kind of like weight training. We found that people can actually build up their compassion 'muscle' and respond to other's suffering with care and a desire to help."[8]

God's word says,

> "'Be kind to one another, tender-hearted, forgiving each other, just as God in Christ also has forgiven you' (Ephesians 4:32)."

Practicing kindness can be simple. Finish a chore for them. If you happen to be folding laundry, grab your child's laundry, fold it, and put the laundry basket on their bed. Make your child's favorite meal. It doesn't have to be fancy; it's the thought that counts.

Another way to get even more benefit from acts of kindness is to enlist your child to do something with you for someone else. This could be kind of exciting, like paying for someone's food at a restaurant. Or it might be something simple, like babysitting for a young mom you know. Your child might like to bake cookies for his class or sports team.

When you practice kindness together toward someone else, you both get a beautiful flow of positive brain chemistry, which is bonding for your relationship.

Tell Your Child Their Story

Narrative storytelling is a powerful way to process things that have happened in our lives. At the beginning of the book, we asked you to remember why you adopted in the first place. But it wasn't the end of the story. We encourage you to tell your child's story to them regularly.

> **Melissa**
> I am one of three children adopted from Korea. Growing up, we celebrated Airplane Day. This is the day an airplane delivered us to our parents. On Airplane Day, we got a special dinner, and then my parents would sit on the sofa with our baby books and tell us our adoption story. Since I was the oldest, my story starts with their battle with infertility and how desperately they wanted children. They told me how excited they were when they first saw my photo. They told me how proud my grandmother was to have "extra special" grandchildren. They showed me an album full of my first photos, with

> each member of my extended family and all my parents' close friends.
>
> Once, I was at a funeral where a lady my parents have known for years told me how vividly she remembers praying for my trip to America. She had mourned with my mom through years of infertility and was so excited to rejoice with her when her prayers were finally answered by my arrival. I even have a quilt my parents' church made to celebrate my arrival. Kids drew photos for me, and the ladies painstakingly embroidered the drawings onto quilt blocks.
>
> While I know every adoptee processes their story differently, I believe the narrative my parents told me helped shape my perspective and my identity. I knew from their storytelling that I was cherished and precious.

You may find it difficult to share your child's story with them. This may be because you're not sure what is developmentally appropriate. You may be afraid of sharing disturbing details and omit information your child needs to know. Or maybe you're not sure how much to share at one time. It's not uncommon that parents can struggle with their feelings toward birth family and might find it hard to speak in a helpful way.

If any of this resonates with you, consider seeking a professional to help you explore your child's story. Even if your child's story is very hard, it needs to be shared with them. As Jayne Schooler says, "They were there."[9] If you don't provide a narrative for your child, they will create one. And it may be worse than what actually happened.

Your relationship with your child may not be what you expected, but you can continue offering connection and building on what you have right now. Remember: you can't control how your child feels or responds, but your efforts are planting seeds and are not wasted.

Reflections and Practices for Chapter 10

Day 1: Establish a Foundation of Fun

Brainstorm some activities your family enjoys. How can you incorporate one new fun thing into your weekly routine? Be creative. Keep it short and sweet. Maybe it's making waffles on Saturday morning or going to the park after school on Fridays. Whatever it is, make sure it's not related to their behavior. Your child doesn't need to earn this fun activity. It happens no matter what.

What will you try?

Day 2: Give an Unexpected "Yes"

Trust us when we say this is a fun activity. Next time your child asks for something you would normally say no to, surprise them by giving an enthusiastic "Yes!"

You may not be able to do this today, since you need to wait for your child to ask, but prepare your mind and heart for the moment when it happens. The results may surprise you.

Take a moment to write about the experience.

Day 3: Regulate Together

Think of activities that are rhythmic, repetitive, and relational, and begin incorporating them into your daily and weekly routines.

Here are some ideas to get you started:

- riding bikes
- throwing a ball back and forth
- chewing gum
- swinging
- rocking in a rocking chair
- jumping rope
- walking
- playing a clapping game

Day 4: Practice Pausing

The next time you encounter a challenging behavior, count to ten before addressing it. In that time, are you able to choose radical compassion and stay curious about the reason behind the behavior? Are you able to respond rather than react?

Write some reflections.

Day 5: Read and Reflect

"My greatest hope for you is that beneath your child's behaviors you'll find the real child, the child who is precious, who wants to connect, who wants desperately to be loved—but who has had to protect their heart from their history."[10]

Conclusion

> **Lisa**
>
> My son crawled wearily into bed, barely pulling the covers around him. "I don't know why I'm so tired," he said as he closed his eyes.
>
> "Probably because you had a full day of school followed by football practice."
>
> "Mm-hmm," he whispered.
>
> I looked at this beautiful boy, on the brink of being a teen, and breathed in, my eyes filling with tears. I love him and I'm so thankful God counted me worthy to be his mom.

We hope this book has encouraged you to take steps toward overcoming blocked care. By filling your internal, external, and relational buckets, you'll find your capacity to choose radical compassion toward your child increase.

As you heal, you will begin looking at your child through a new lens. One day, a beautiful thing may happen. You'll see your child with all their challenges and feel something shift in your heart. Empathy will be awakened.

Adoption is complicated. You stepped into brokenness, with hearts longing to bring wholeness to your children. It's the hardest thing we've ever done. Maybe you feel the same. We both thought we had what it would take to parent our children. We were confident in our ability.

We were wrong.

Thankfully, we know the One who does have what it takes. In fact, He has it all. We turn to God again and again as we parent our kids, and He pours out peace and grace. We both spend a lot more time praying and trusting now than we did when we were younger. Adoption and foster care revealed our brokenness in unexpected ways. Our hearts are examined and found wanting, which is ultimately good news because we find ourselves once again in need of Jesus.

So much loss, and love, and sorrow, and joy. Yet, we wouldn't miss it for the world.

This is not a quick fix. Overcoming blocked care and finding your way back to compassionate and connected parenting takes time and intention. The new neural pathways in your brain and your child's brain will grow stronger over time with many repetitions.

On the next page, you'll find a second blocked care assessment. It's the same one you completed as you began reading this book. It's time to take the assessment once again to reflect on change and progress.

As you press on in this incredible calling, lean on Jesus. Lean hard and draw strength from Him. He loves you so much, and He loves your kids too. He will give you the courage and endurance to become the parent you want to be.

Thank you for letting us be a part of your healing journey. We firmly believe you can reclaim compassion for your child and yourself. You can heal from blocked care and find empathy rekindled in your heart. We hope you're experiencing it even now.

Remember: you're a good parent doing good work.

Our hearts are with you.

—Lisa and Melissa

Post-reading Assessment

Now that you've completed the book and done the end-of-chapter reflections and practices, let's see where you are today.

Please respond with one of the following: 1—Never, 2—Rarely, 3—Sometimes, 4—Often, 5—Always

I'm too caught up in coping with my child's behavior to be curious about the meaning behind it.	1 2 3 4 5
I feel defensive and guard myself from rejection.	1 2 3 4 5
I feel burned out, chronically overwhelmed, and fatigued.	1 2 3 4 5
I feel resentment toward one or more of my children or my situation as a whole. I may even regret adopting or fostering.	1 2 3 4 5
I feel irritable with other family and friends.	1 2 3 4 5
I isolate myself.	1 2 3 4 5
I'm cynical about helpful ideas.	1 2 3 4 5

I've lost compassion, which has led to shame.	1 2 3 4 5
I've experienced a crisis of faith or challenge of a personal belief system.	1 2 3 4 5
I don't feel real pleasure in parenting.	1 2 3 4 5

NOTES

Introduction

1. Jonathan Baylin and Daniel A. Hughes, *The Neurobiology of Attachment-Focused Therapy: Enhancing Connection and Trust in the Treatment of Children and Adolescents.* (New York, NY: W. W. Norton & Company, 2016), Kindle edition, 77.

Chapter 1: Recognize Your Motivations and Expectations

1. Karyn Purvis PhD and Lisa Qualls, *The Connected Parent: Real-Life Strategies for Building Trust and Attachment*, read by Lisa Qualls, (Eugene, OR: Harvest House Publishers, 2020), Audible audio ed., 4 hrs., 42 min.
2. Deborah D. Gray, *Attaching in Adoption: Practical Tools for Today's Parents* (Philadelphia, PA: Jessica Kingsley Publishers, 2012), 308.
3. Brother Roger of Taizé, "Short Meditation of the Day," Short meditation of the day—Taizé, January 23, 2022, https://www.taize.fr/en_article75.html?date=2022-01–23.

Chapter 2: Acknowledge Shame and Grief

1. Pauline Boss, *Ambiguous Loss: Learning to Live with Unresolved Grief* (Cambridge, MA: Harvard University Press, 2000).
2. Lisa S. Zoll, LCSW, "Disenfranchised Grief: When Grief and Grievers Are Unrecognized," The New Social Worker, December 27, 2018, https://www.socialworker.com/feature-articles/

practice/disenfranchised-grief-when-grief-and-grievers-are-unrecogniz/.
3. Elisabeth Kubler-Ross, *On Death and Dying: What the Dying Have to Teach Doctors, Nurses, Clergy and Their Own Families,* (New York, NY: Scribner, 2011), retrieved from https://www.scribd.com/read/224314500/On-Death-and-Dying.
4. David Kessler, *Finding Meaning: The Sixth Stage of Grief,* (New York, NY: Scribner, 2019).
5. Dane C. Ortlund, *Gentle and Lowly: The Heart of Christ for Sinners and Sufferers* (Wheaton, IL: Crossway Book, 2020), 178–179.

Chapter 3: Understand Blocked Trust

1. Jon Baylin, PhD and Dan Hughes, PhD, "Children's Blocked Trust: How Compassionate Care Helps Reverse the Effects of Early Poor Care," The North American Council on Adoptable Children, July 2, 2018, https://nacac.org/resource/childrens-blocked-trust-how-compassionate-care-helps-reverse-the-effects-of-early-poor-care/.
2. Baylin, PhD and Hughes, PhD, "Children's Blocked Trust."
3. Baylin, PhD and Hughes, PhD, "Children's Blocked Trust."
4. Dyadic Developmental Psychotherapy Institute, "How early years trauma affects the brain the child who mistrusts good care HD," February 15, 2016, YouTube Video, 11:20, https://www.youtube.com/watch?v=xuRagD9ES9w.
5. Dyadic Developmental Psychotherapy Institute, "Early years trauma," 15:09.

Chapter 4: Understand Blocked Care

1. Baylin and Hughes, *The Neurobiology of Attachment-Focused Therapy*, 74.

2. Jonathan F. Baylin and Daniel A. Hughes, *Brain-Based Parenting: The Neuroscience of Caregiving for Healthy Attachment* (New York, NY: Norton, 2012), 99.
3. Baylin and Hughes, *Brain-Based Parenting*, 83.
4. Desmond Tutu, "Nobel Peace Prize Laureate" (lecture, Oslo City Hall, Norway, December 10, 1984).

Part 3: Overcome Blocked Care

1. Baylin, PhD and Hughes, PhD, "Children's Blocked Trust."
2. James Clear, *Atomic Habits: An Easy & Proven Way to Build Good Habits & Break Bad Ones* (New York, NY: Avery, 2018).
3. Clear, *Atomic Habits*, 74.

Chapter 5: Be Kind to Your Body

1. Water Science School, "The Water in You: Water and the Human Body," USGS, May 22, 2019, https://www.usgs.gov/special-topics/water-science-school/science/water-you-water-and-human-body?qt-science_center_objects=0#qt-science_center_objects.
2. Gilles Berrut and Patrick Ritz, "The Importance of Good Hydration for Day-to-Day Health," *Nutrition Reviews* 63 (June 2005), https://doi.org/10.1111/j.1753-4887.2005.tb00155.x.
3. Gina Shaw, "Water and Your Diet: Staying Slim and Regular With H2O," Nourish by WebMD, February 13, 2022, https://www.webmd.com/diet/features/water-for-weight-loss-diet#1.
4. Arianne Missimer, "Vagus Nerve Hack: Pelvic Floor Relaxation," The Movement Paradigm, August 9, 2021, https://themovementparadigm.com/pelvic-floor-relaxation/.
5. Marie C Béné, Jean-François Bisson, and Patrizia A. d'Alessio, "Anti-Stress Effects of d-Limonene and Its Metabolite Perillyl Alcohol," Rejuvenation Research 17, no. 2 (April 17, 2014), pp. 145-149, https://doi.org/10.1089/rej.2013.1515.

6. Megan O'Neill Melle, "Need More Motivation to Exercise? Here Are 6 Mental Benefits," Parade, April 15, 2022, https://parade.com/979263/meganoneill/mental-benefits-of-exercise/.
7. Bessel van der Kolk MD, *The Body Keeps the Score: Brain, Mind, and Body in the Healing of Trauma* (New York, NY: Penguin Publishing Group, 2015).

Chapter 6: Establish a Healthy Mindset

1. Max Lucado, "Leaving Your Concerns with God," Max Lucado, July 13, 2021, https://maxlucado.com/watch/leaving-your-concerns-with-god/.
2. Emiliana R. Simon-Thomas, PhD, "A "Thnx" a Day Keeps the Doctor Away," Greater Good Magazine, December 19, 2012, https://greatergood.berkeley.edu/article/item/a_thnx_a_day_keeps_the_doctor_away.
3. Katie Davis Majors, *Daring to Hope: Finding God's Goodness in the Broken and the Beautiful* (New York, NY: Multnomah, 2018), 16.
4. Daniel Hughes PhD, "Creating PACE for the special children in our lives," Daniel Hughes, http://www.danielhughes.org/p.a.c.e..html.
5. Dr. Karyn Purvis, "Give Your Child Playfulness," Empowered to Connect, March 20, 2011, https://empoweredtoconnect.org/give-your-child-playfulness.
6. Paul Osincup, "Leading with Laughter: The Power of Humor in Leadership | Paul Osincup | TEDxNapaValley," May 31, 2016, YouTube Video, 7:45, https://www.youtube.com/watch?v=yhokMZdQ7gs.
7. Christina Congleton, Britta K. Hölzel, and Sara W. Lazar, "Mindfulness Can Literally Change Your Brain," Harvard Business Review, January 8, 2015, https://hbr.org/2015/01/mindfulness-can-literally-change-your-brain.

8. University of Waterloo, "Just 10 minutes of meditation helps anxious people have better focus," ScienceDaily, May 1, 2017, https://sciencedaily.com/releases/2017/05/170501094325.htm.
9. Kendra Adachi, "10 Ways to Beast Your Monday," The Lazy Genius Collective, January 30, 2017, https://www.thelazygeniuscollective.com/blog/beast-your-monday.
10. Srini Pillay, "Your Brain Can Only Take So Much Focus," Harvard Business Review, May 12, 2017, https://hbr.org/2017/05/your-brain-can-only-take-so-much-focus.
11. Majors, *Daring to Hope,* 43.

Chapter 7: Immerse Yourself in Comfort and Beauty

1. Jo L. Barton, Daniel K. Brown, and Valerie F. Gladwell, "Viewing Nature Scenes Positively Affects Recovery of Autonomic Function Following Acute-Mental Stress," *Environmental Science & Technology* 47, no. 11 (June 4, 2013): pp. 5562-5569, https://doi.org/10.1021/es305019p.
2. Stephen W. Porges, *The Pocket Guide to the Polyvagal Theory: The Transformative Power of Feeling Safe,* (New York, NY: W. W. Norton & Company, 2017), 86.
3. Lutz Jäncke and Stefan Koelsc, "Music and the Heart," *European Heart Journal* 36, no. 44 (November 21, 2015): pp. 3043-3049, https://doi.org/10.1093/eurheartj/ehv430.
4. Ann Bonnema, *Creative God.* Live Today Well Collective. 2022.

Chapter 8: Lean into God

1. Paul E. Miller, *A Praying Life: Connecting with God in a Distracting World* (Colorado Springs, CO: NavPress, 2017), 24.
2. Miller, *A Praying Life,* 25.
3. Ruth Haley Barton, *Invitation to Solitude and Silence: Experiencing God's Transforming,* read by author, (Carol Stream, IL: Oasis Audio, 2009), Audible audio ed., 4 hr., 8 min.

Chapter 9: Surround Yourself with Life-Giving People

1. Bruce D. Perry and Oprah Winfrey, *What Happened to You?: Conversations on Trauma, Resilience, and Healing,* read by authors, (New York, NY: Macmillan Audio, 2021), Audible audio ed., 8 hrs., 27 min.
2. Bryan and Rachel Hehr. "Is Spiritual Formation Navel-Gazing?," Curative Ministries, February 8, 2022, https://curateministries.org/curateblog/2022/2/8/is-spiritual-formation-navel-gazing.
3. Deb Dana, *Anchored: How to Befriend Your Nervous System Using Polyvagal Theory,* (Louisville, CO: Sounds True, 2021), retrieved from https://www.scribd.com/read/529068336/Anchored-How-to-Befriend-Your-Nervous-System-Using-Polyvagal-Theory.

Chapter 10: Connect with Your Child

1. Dr. Bruce Perry, "Born for Love: Why Empathy is Endangered – and Essential," May 15, 2014, YouTube video, 28:15 to 34:17, https://www.youtube.com/watch?v=M6kDeBaJioM
2. Mona Delahooke, *Beyond Behaviors: Using Brain Science and Compassion to Understand and Solve Children's Behavioral Challenges,* (Eau Claire, WI: PESI Publishing & Media, 2019), Kindle edition, 264.
3. Bruce D. Perry and Maia Szalavitz, *Born for Love: Why Empathy Is Essential--and Endangered,* (New York, NY: HarperCollins, 2011), retrieved from https://www.scribd.com/book/163599729/Born-for-Love-Why-Empathy-Is-Essential-and-Endangered.
4. Stephanie Watson, "Oxytocin: The love hormone," Harvard Health Publishing, July 20, 2021, https://www.health.harvard.edu/mind-and-mood/oxytocin-the-love-hormone.

5. Rick Chillot, "The Power of Touch," Psychology Today, March 11, 2013, https://www.psychologytoday.com/us/articles/201303/the-power-touch.
6. Steve Siegle, L.P.C., "The art of kindness," Mayo Clinic Health System. May 20, 2020, https://www.mayoclinichealthsystem.org/hometown-health/speaking-of-health/the-art-of-kindness.
7. Cedars-Sinai Staff, "The Science of Kindness," Cedars Sinai, February 13, 2019, https://www.cedars-sinai.org/blog/science-of-kindness.html.
8. Cedars-Sinai Staff, "The Science of Kindness."
9. Jayne Schooler, "Telling the Truth to Your Child: Helping Your Child Come to a Strength-Based Understanding of His Story," Focus on the Family, June 29, 2020, https://www.focusonthefamily.com/pro-life/telling-the-truth/.
10. Purvis and Qualls, *The Connected Parent*.

Acknowledgements

Deepest thanks to the adoptive parents who share their lives with us; you are the reason this book was written. Thank you for asking the questions that led us down this road of research and writing. We are firm believers in the power of community to help people heal; thank you for being part of ours.

Dr. Jonathan Baylin and Dr. Daniel Hughes, you gave us words for what we witnessed in ourselves and other adoptive parents. We are grateful for your research and work, which benefit the families we serve.

Thank you to friends who kindly read our earliest version of this book and offered suggestions to make it much better. Megan Clarke, Jessica Sinarski, Greg Lombard Rea, Autumn Knapp, Nakole Wooley, and Risa Forrester, we appreciate you.

Jessica Choi, your superb editing skills pushed us to write a better book than we could possibly have produced on our own. We are grateful for you.

Leah Kent, you took our words and ideas and created a beautiful book we're proud to share with the world. Thank you.

To our families, we promise we'll start cooking dinner again soon. Thank you for giving us space to devote many hours to this project and for believing we had something important to offer adoptive families.

And to the One who made our paths cross despite living more than 3,000 miles apart, we're still in awe of what you've led us to create. Thank you for leading us to serve adoptive families. God, we love you with all our hearts, souls, and strength and aspire to love our neighbors as ourselves.

About the Authors

Lisa C. Qualls

Lisa C. Qualls is the author of *The Connected Parent* (with Dr. Karyn Purvis), a TBRI Practitioner, and a Christian spiritual director. As a birth mom and adoptive mom, she writes and speaks with wisdom about the challenges and beauty of adoption. Lisa and her husband Russ live in Idaho and have twelve children and two granddaughters.

Melissa Corkum

As an adoptee and adoptive mom, Melissa Corkum provides insight and resources to adoptees and their parents through her writing, coaching, and speaking. She is a Safe and Sound Protocol Practitioner and Certified Enneagram Coach. Melissa and her husband, Patrick, live in Maryland and have six kids and two grandchildren.

Together, they serve thousands of adoptive parents by providing post-adoption support through their podcast, books, speaking, and coaching.

To learn more, find Lisa and Melissa at
www.reclaimcompassion.com

Made in United States
Orlando, FL
18 April 2023

32239562R00145